Matthew Willis

Colour illustrations by Chris Sandham-Bailey

Fai[illegible]y FLYCATCHER

STRATUS

STRATUS sp.j.
Po. Box 123,
27-600 Sandomierz 1, Poland
e-mail: office@mmpbooks.biz
for
Mushroom Model Publications,
3 Gloucester Close, Petersfield,
Hampshire GU32 3AX, UK.
E-mail: rogerw@mmpbooks.biz

http://www.mmpbooks.biz

ISBN
978-83-63678-92-0

Editor in chief
Roger Wallsgrove

Editorial Team
Bartłomiej Belcarz
Artur Juszczak
James Kightly
Robert Pęczkowski

DTP
Stratus s.c

Colour Drawings
Chris Sandham-Bailey

Scale Plans
Dariusz Karnas

Printed by:
Drukarnia Diecezjalna,
ul. Żeromskiego 4,
27-600 Sandomierz

PRINTED IN POLAND

Table of contents

Cover and title page photo: *Fairey Flycatchers N9922/'5', N9954/'7' and N9923/'1' of 402 Flight, HMS* Eagle. *(Photograph from the Fleet Air Arm Museum's collection)*

Acknowledgements

The author would like to express his gratitude to the following individuals and organisations, without whose support and help this book would not have been possible: Barbara Gilbert and Catherine Cooper at the Fleet Air Arm Museum's archive for their help with documents and photographs held by the museum; Steve Moorey, Adrian Balch, Archive Images and Andy Pym for the generous permission to use photographs from their collections, and Philip Jarrett for his advice; Nick Stroud of The Aviation Historian for originally commissioning the piece of work on the Flycatcher that led to this book, and for that publication's commitment to the less obvious aspects of aviation history. The author would also like to thank MMP Books for their support, and, last but not least, Rosalind, for allowing him to sit at home all day and write about aeroplanes.

Introduction

No aircraft is more evocative of British naval aviation between the wars than the Fairey Flycatcher. The idiosyncratic biplane was loved by crews and public alike despite its unlikely appearance and relatively pedestrian performance. Famed more for its aerobatic prowess and public demonstrations than glory on the field of battle, there can be few warplanes that are so closely associated with peacetime. If the RAF between the wars was the 'world's finest flying club', then the Fleet Air Arm was unquestionably its yachting branch – and the Flycatcher was the perfect mount for expressing the youthful high spirits of its members.

The Flycatcher was agile yet forgiving, and the perfect deck-landing type in an era before effective arrester gear was developed. It was also tough and reliable. It was these characteristics which made it one of the most popular naval aircraft in British history. Even its odd appearance seemed endearing rather than ugly, and the bright, colourful inter-war markings enthusiastically adopted by front-line Fighter Flights added to the aircraft's visual appeal.

The Flycatcher was never engaged in a war, though it was taken into some potentially dangerous situations through the FAA's 'colonial policing' of trouble spots in the British Empire. It served the Royal Navy doing everything from tackling pirates off the Chinese coast to entertaining crowds at Schneider Trophy events with aerobatic displays. The generation of pilots that flew Flycatchers in active service is no longer with us, but the 1934 'Aviation Memoirs' of Owen Cathcart-Jones provides a fascinating glimpse into life in a Flycatcher Flight in the 1920s. Cathcart-Jones' reminiscences are quoted throughout this book.

Furthermore, while there are no surviving original Flycatchers, a replica was built in the 1970s by a member of the Fairey family, and which aimed to replicate as closely as possible the performance and handling of the original. The replica, which has since retired from flying and can be seen in the Fleet Air Arm Museum, provided an invaluable insight into the Flycatcher's flying characteristics.

Despite fewer than 200 Flycatchers being built, the type served as the Fleet Air Arm's sole fighter for the best part of a decade. It had its roots in the concepts and designs of the First World War but was still in service when specifications leading to the Second World War Blackburn Skua and Fairey Fulmar were being drawn up.

The Flycatcher served as the main British naval fighter for most of its life and bridged the long gap between First World War technology and thinking, and the cantilever monoplane era. It eclipsed its competitors and defied several attempts at replacement. So comprehensively did the Flycatcher put its stamp on pre-war naval flying that it is easy to overlook the fact that it very nearly lost out to the Parnall Plover as the main British naval fighter. Equally, it seems surprising today that, at the time, the Fairey fighter was only intended to occupy this role for two or three years, after which time it was expected that substantially better equipment would be available.

Genesis and Development

A need for renewal

By the end of the First World War Britain had rapidly built an almost unassailable lead in naval aviation, particularly in the use of shipboard fighters and fighter bombers. The Tondern Raid in July 1918, where Sopwith Camels flying from HMS *Furious* had destroyed two Zeppelins and damaged hangars, had proved the potential of carrier-borne landplanes to project striking power. Specialist carrier aircraft were commissioned to develop this capability, such as the Sopwith Cuckoo torpedo bomber and Port Victoria Grain Griffin reconnaissance bomber, as well as derivatives of existing types like the Sopwith 2F1 'Ship's Camel' and the Sopwith 'Pup'-derived Beardmore S.B.3D/F.

In the years immediately following the war, however, the Royal Navy's lead in the development and use of aircraft carriers was almost completely thrown away. The transfer of naval aviation to the RAF together with peacetime economies had, by 1921, left the RN with only one operational aircraft carrier, HMS *Argus*, and but a handful of aircraft.

The almost total slump in carrier aviation was untenable, and soon the Admiralty began to take steps to address the matter with several additional aircraft-carrying ships – another three carriers and a seaplane-carrying cruiser would be available by the mid-1920s.

Further strength in aircraft was clearly necessary to complement the increase in ships. Only one naval fighter had entered service since the war, the unsuccessful Nieuport Nightjar, of which a mere 22 had been constructed, to a WW1 era design derived from the Nighthawk fighter. This, despite its manufacturer's Gallic name, was a British aircraft designed by H.P. Folland in 1918 for the Nieuport and General company, the licence-producer of the French manufacturer's designs in the UK. The Nighthawk had, like so many aircraft developed in 1918-19, been left without its designed engine by the debacle of the ABC Dragonfly radial, with the result that when the modified Nightjar appeared, the only suitable powerplant was the 230 hp rotary Bentley BR2. The use of a powerful rotary engine was likely to have contributed to the Nightjar's nasty tendency to flick into a spin on final approach, which rendered it completely unsuitable for naval use. A number were lost in fatal accidents during deck-landing training.

Against this background, in 1921 the Air Ministry and the Admiralty created a specification for a single-seat deck-landing fighter. The requirement was challenging. The fighter would be required to operate from land bases, aircraft carriers and launching platforms on other warships. It had to be readily convertible from landplane configuration to floatplane or amphibian. It had to incorporate alternative engine types, and be armed with machine guns and bombs. Naturally, the aircraft must have a good performance and endurance, and must be stable and safe to land aboard an aircraft carrier. Needless to say, many of these characteristics were not entirely complementary and meeting them all would stretch contemporary design to the limit.

One factor which would make the development of a new aircraft possible was the promise of new air-cooled engines developing 350–400 hp, the Armstrong Siddeley Jaguar 14-cylinder two-row radial, and the Bristol Jupiter nine-cylinder single-row radial. These engines had been under development for a number of years, starting life as the Royal Aircraft Factory RAF.8 and the Brazil Straker/Cosmos Jupiter respectively, and were by 1921 near to reaching production standard. Although liquid-cooled engines such as the Napier Lion were then available, for the time being these would be unsuitable for fighters of the kind the Admiralty required, being too big and heavy to allow sufficiently short take-offs and landings. The Admiralty had something of a preference for the Jupiter, which was then the more powerful of the two engines, though it was also heavier than the Jaguar, and both engines would be considered.

The competitors

Fairey was not the only company to be asked to provide prototypes to meet the requirement, nor even the first. George Parnall and Company was given a contract for three aircraft on the 8th March 1922, three days before Fairey was given a similar contract.

Fairey had some experience with aircraft for the Navy, but almost all of this was with floatplanes. The large Campania reconnaissance bomber had been purpose-designed for use aboard seaplane carriers – useful experience that was still somewhat different from continuous-deck aircraft carrier operations.

The company had however designed the 'Fairey Patent Camber Changing Gear', one of the first practical applications of the trailing edge flap. This shortened the landing and take-off, and improved the load that could be carried. This had been used on the single-seat Hamble Baby floatplane, a development of the Sopwith Baby. The adjustable camber had been useful chiefly to enable the Baby to lift off the water when heavily loaded, but another useful characteristic of the system was to reduce landing speed – a huge benefit in a deck-landing aircraft. (It could also be tuned to reduce drag by raising the trailing edge slightly from the 'neutral' position). A number of Hamble Baby aircraft were rebuilt with landplane undercarriage and were used for training, though it was mooted that they might be suitable for use aboard HMS *Argus*, the first continuous-deck carrier, which was commissioned just before the end of the First World War; in the event, more modern designs were utilized aboard the early aircraft carriers.

Despite Fairey's credentials with naval aircraft, on the face of it at least, Parnall had the advantage. The company had already designed and built a dedicated carrier aircraft, the Panther fleet spotter, of which over 150 had been ordered. Furthermore, Parnall had been responsible for creating the landplane variant of Fairey's Hamble Baby floatplane which had been considered as a possible carrier fighter during WW1. This had given

The first Flycatcher prototype was N163, seen here probably at Gosport during service trials, in an Air Ministry photograph dated 17 March 1923. Flycatcher N163 had first flown at Hamble on 28 November 1922. It spent most of its career in trials, particularly during the competition with the Parnall Plover to select the Fleet Air Arm single-seat fighter. (Author's collection)

A close-up of the Flycatcher first prototype's undercarriage, built around Fairey patent oleo-pneumatic struts, and which gave the Flycatcher its characteristic 'kneeling' appearance. The undercarriage was one of the aircraft's most successful features, being perfectly suited to the tough treatment it received in deck landings. (Author's collection)

the company a close look at the workings of Fairey's camber-changing gear. In response to the specification, the Bristol-based company created the Plover, a biplane with a similar plywood-skinned structure to the Panther.

The experience with the Panther had given the company considerable insight into the challenges of producing an aircraft which could effectively operate from a carrier, stand up to the rigours of use in rough seas and high winds, and remain serviceable on long cruises.

The design Fairey submitted naturally owed a great deal to the Hamble Baby – the wings and tail were of very similar planform, for example. Nevertheless, the company had given a great deal of thought to the problems posed by the specification, and the results were innovative. The structure was cutting-edge for the times – as John Fairey, who built a flying replica of the Flycatcher in the 1980s, noted, "for an aircraft which first flew in 1922, the Flycatcher

Flycatcher prototype N163 at RAF Northolt where it completed comparative trials with the Parnall Plover in 1924. The adjustable gun bracket is fitted, but no gun is installed. The aircraft still wears its spinner and cowling ring. (Author's collection)

Another view of N163 dated 17 March 1923, with an unknown member of RAF personnel. The unaerodynamic installation of the port .303 in Vickers machine gun with its synchronisation gear and adjustable bracket is clearly visible. Shortly after this photograph was taken, N163 returned to Fairey Hayes division to have its Armstrong-Siddeley Jaguar engine replaced with a Bristol Jupiter, with which it saw out its life. (Author's collection)

contains a great deal of metal",[1] and that it was "a much more advanced aircraft than a First World War Fighter".[2] The design was a modular structure intended to make it easy to replace large sub-assemblies. The 'backbone' of the aircraft was a tubular steel forward fuselage framework integrated with the engine mount, cabane struts and upper wing centre section, including pressed steel wing ribs. Possibly uniquely in biplane design, the Flycatcher had a pronounced, 4° dihedral on its upper wing and none on the lower, making yet another visually unusual feature.

The rear fuselage was a wooden space-frame — parallel longerons were braced not with conventional frames but constant-length uprights and diamond-form struts. Unusually, all the bracing in the vertical units was achieved with wooden members and no wire was used. The result was a very strong structure with a great deal of commonality in the individual components. It eliminated the need to carry a large stock of differing spares, and also simplified the process of trueing the fuselage with tensioning wires.

The 'patent camber-changing gear' remained in a refined form, operated via a crank beneath the instrument panel.

The full-width flaps of the camber-changing gear also acted as ailerons — turning the crank increased the angle of the surfaces while retaining their independent movement as ailerons. This was achieved with a closed-loop circuit of control wires operated in the normal way by the control column; the column was itself mounted on a lever which was raised and lowered using a worm screw, which lowered the trailing edges of all four ailerons down while maintaining the correct tension in the circuit. It allowed infinite adjustment between

1. Fairey, J.S., Flycatcher Facsimile (part 1), Aeroplane Monthly March 1982 p.131.
2. Fairey, J.S., Flycatcher Facsimile (part 1), Aeroplane Monthly March 1982 p.130.

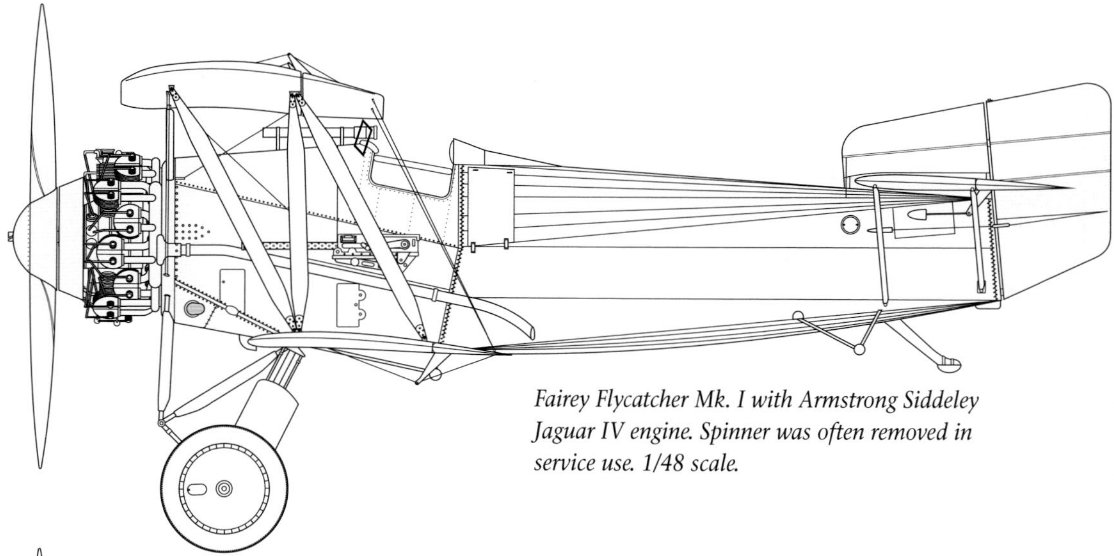

Fairey Flycatcher Mk. I with Armstrong Siddeley Jaguar IV engine. Spinner was often removed in service use. 1/48 scale.

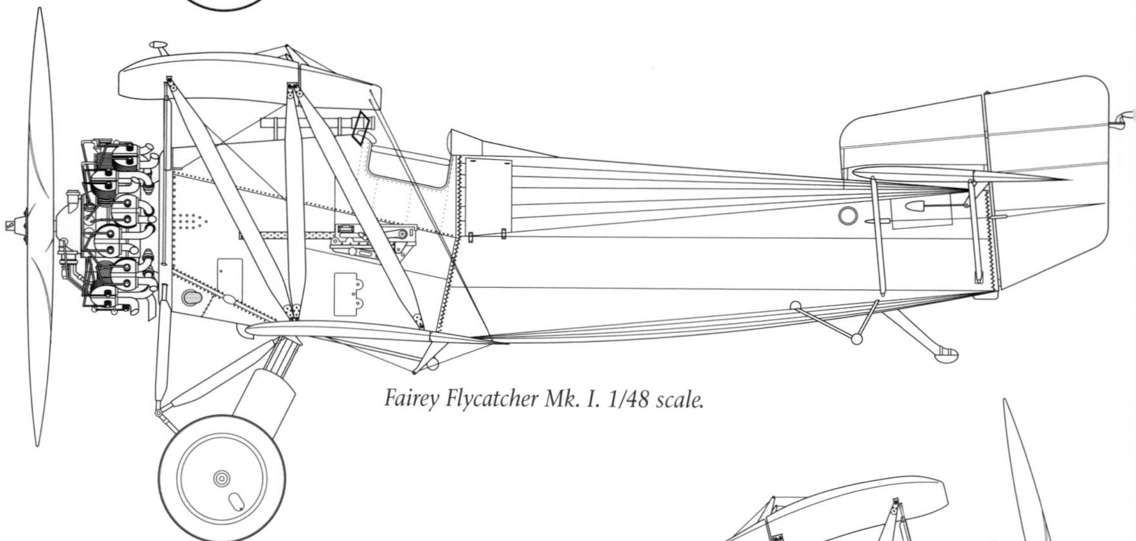

Fairey Flycatcher Mk. I. 1/48 scale.

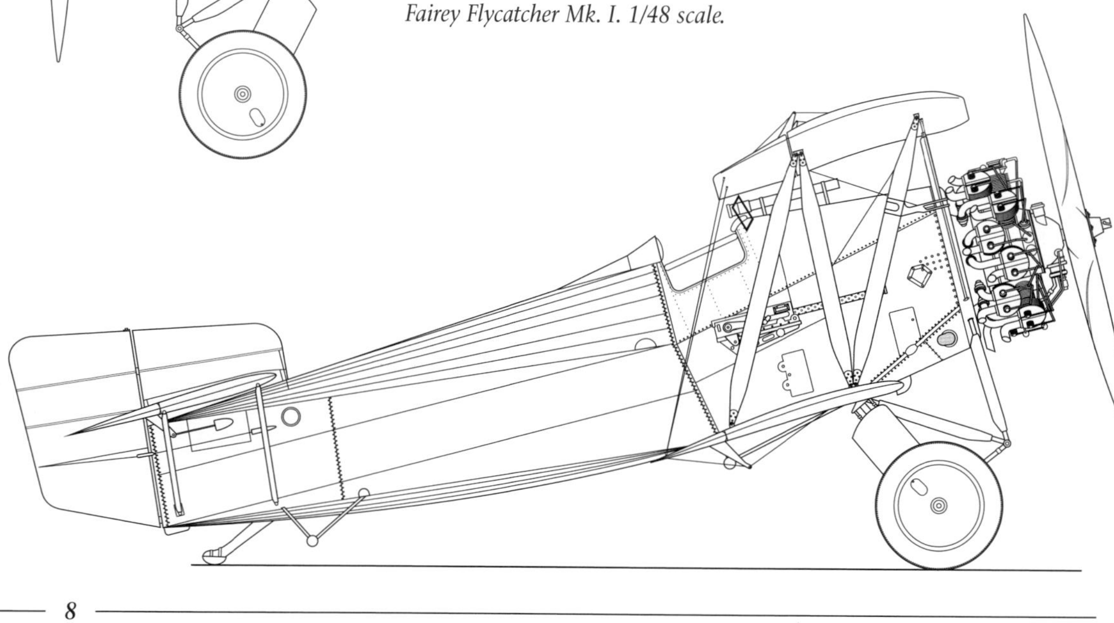

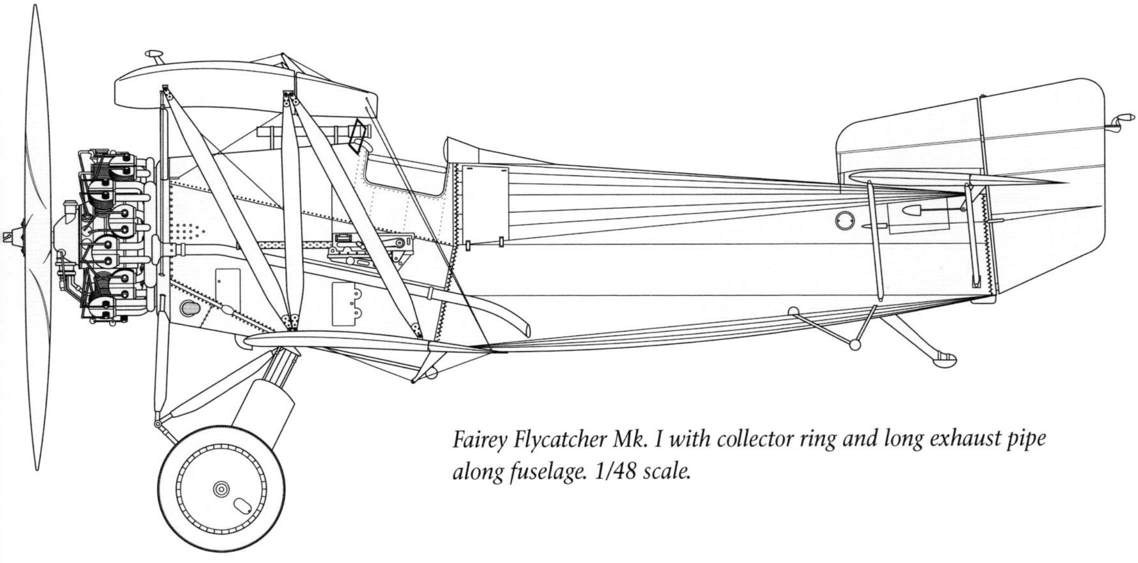

Fairey Flycatcher Mk. I with collector ring and long exhaust pipe along fuselage. 1/48 scale.

Fairey badge.

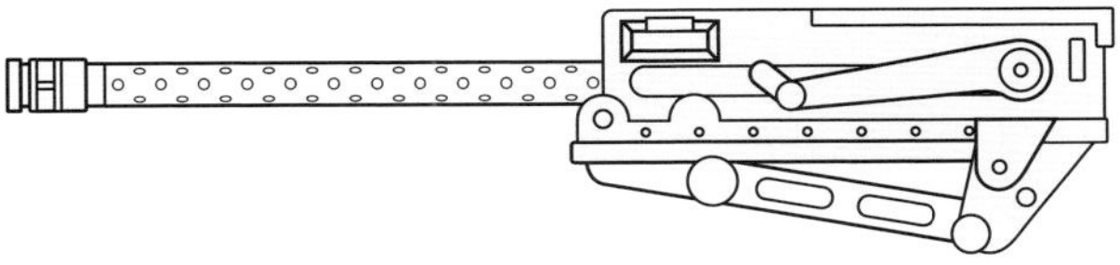

Vickers machine gun. (Not to scale)

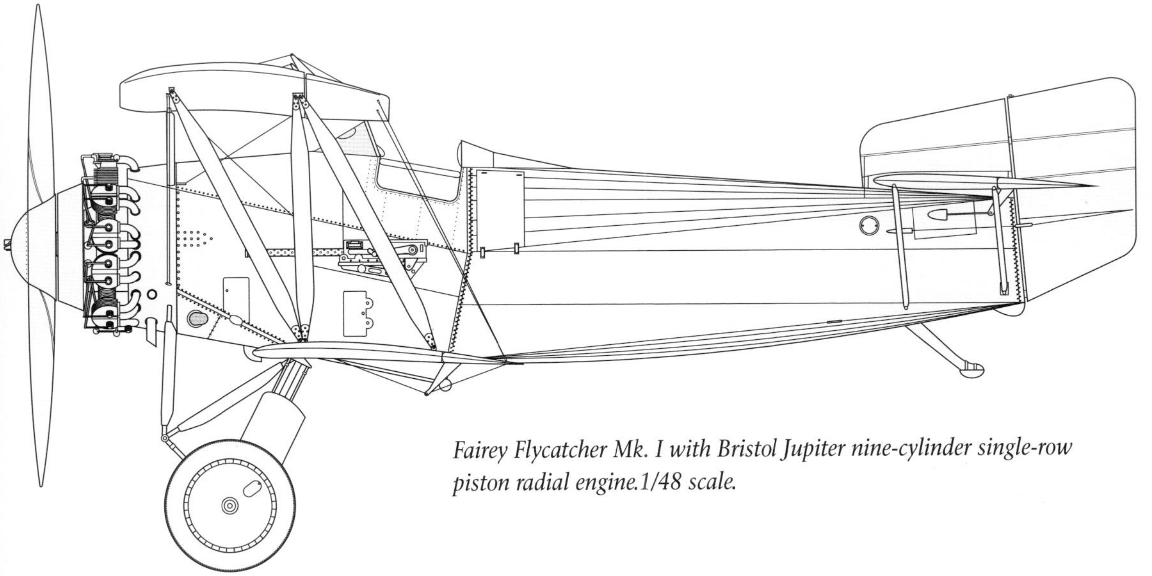

Fairey Flycatcher Mk. I with Bristol Jupiter nine-cylinder single-row piston radial engine.1/48 scale.

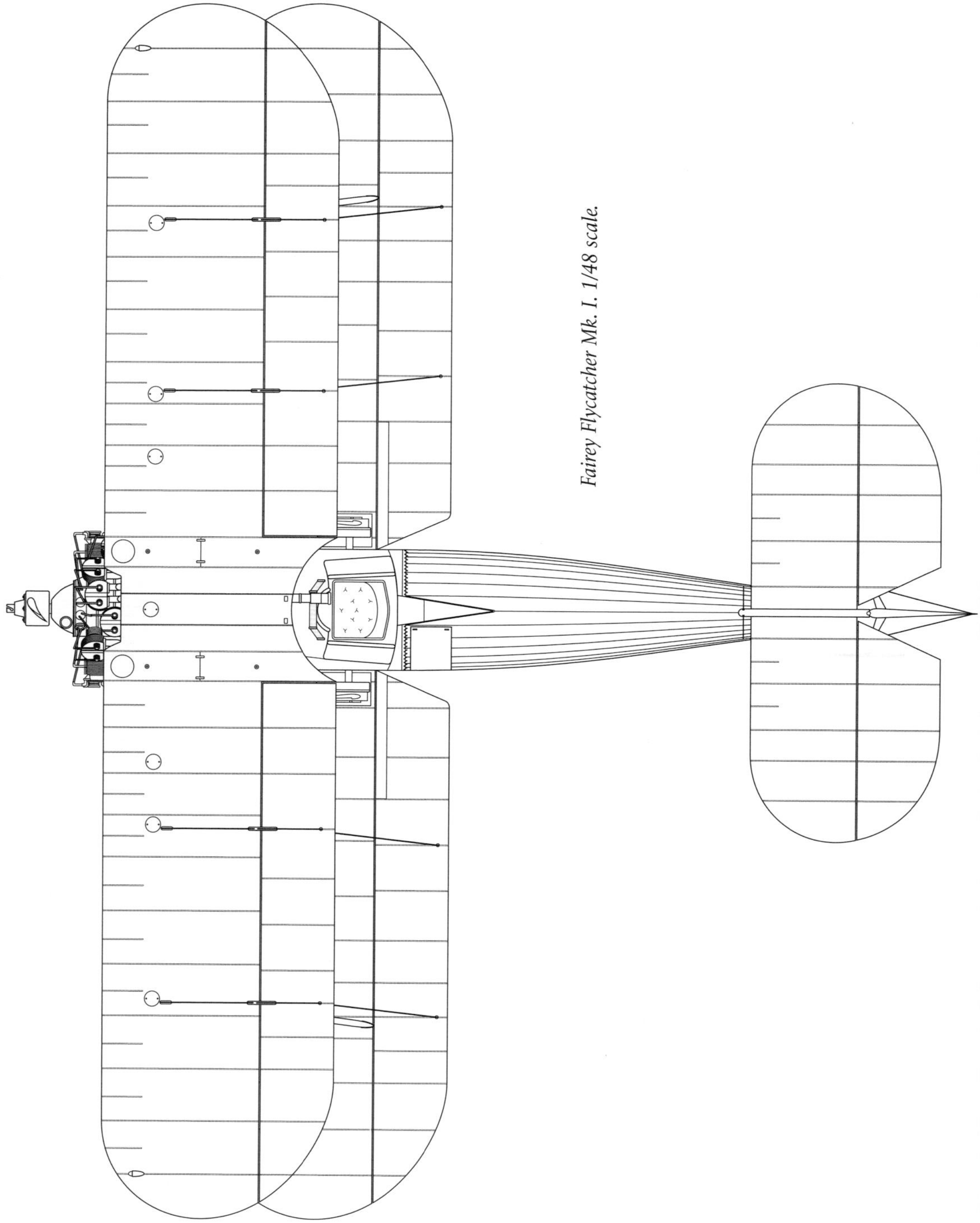

Fairey Flycatcher Mk. I. 1/48 scale.

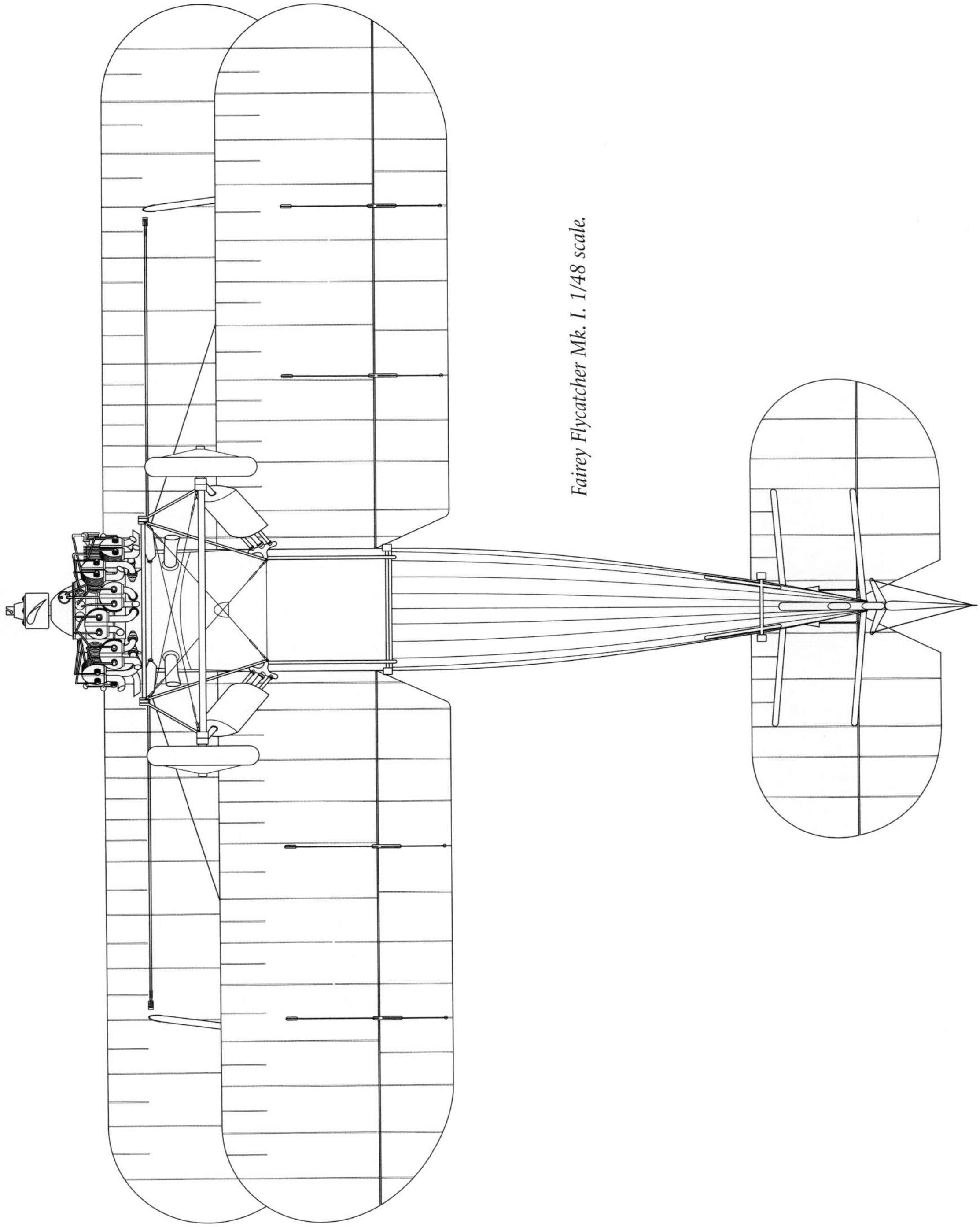

Fairey Flycatcher Mk. I. 1/48 scale.

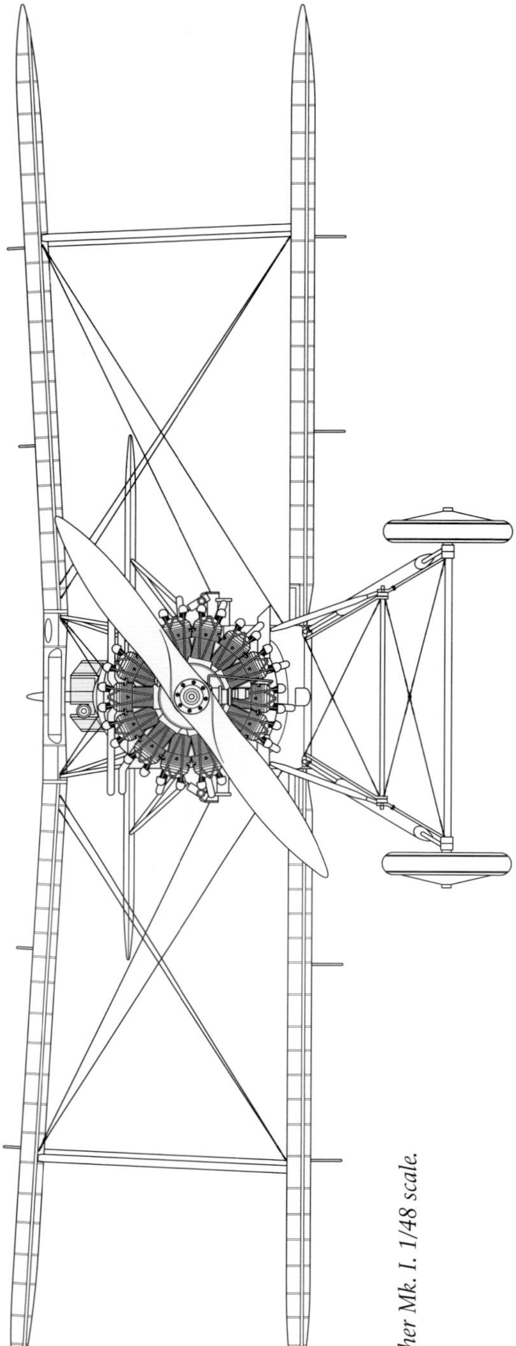

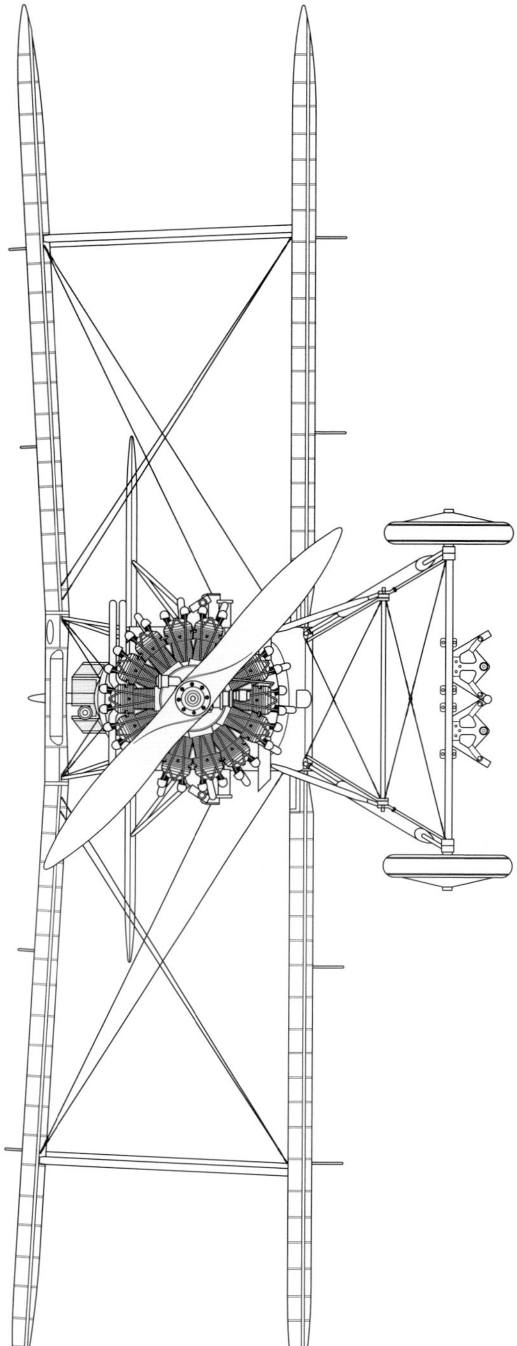

Fairey Flycatcher Mk. I. 1/48 scale.

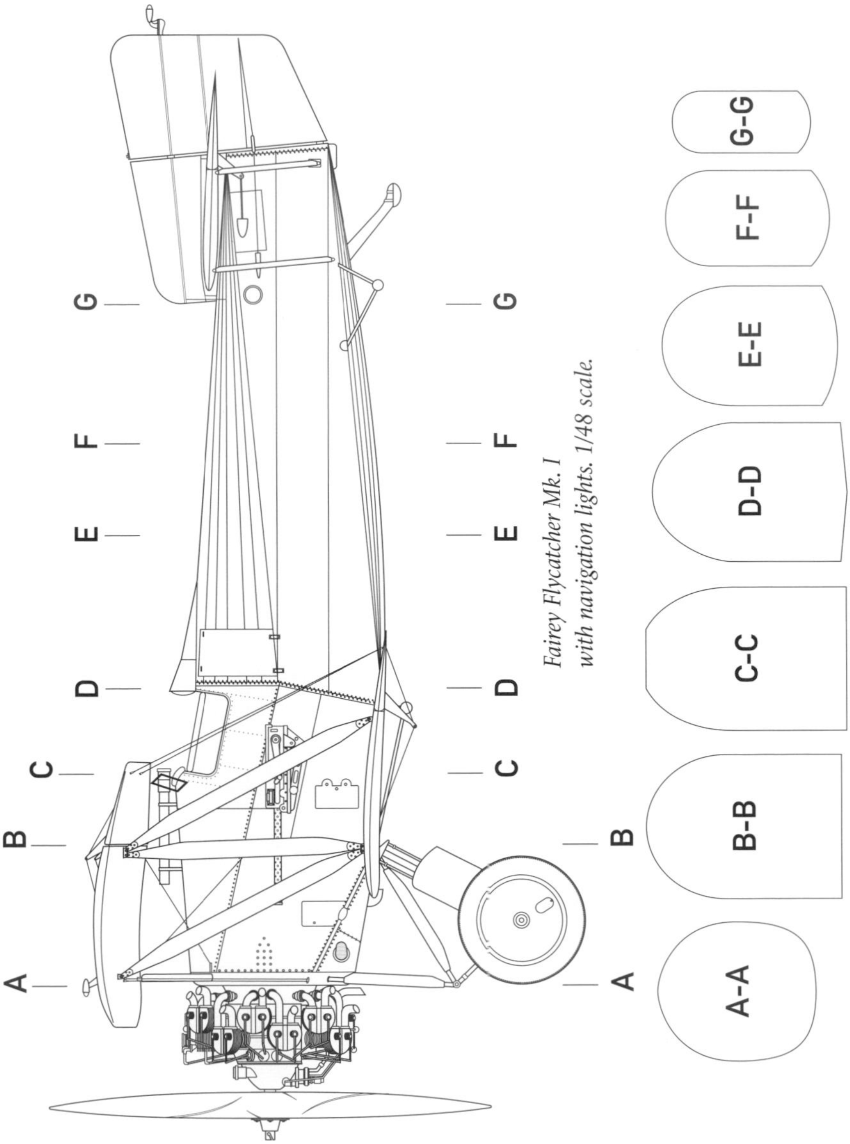

Fairey Flycatcher Mk. I
with navigation lights. 1/48 scale.

The second prototype Fairey Flycatcher was N164, which first flew on 5 May 1923. The aircraft was mainly used in experimental and test flying, including fuel consumption tests, trials of an experimental cowling, deck-landing trials, tests of a more powerful Jaguar engine and float releasing gear. The aircraft was in most respects identical to N163, but here appears to have a smaller tail fin than the standard item. (Author's collection)

The third Flycatcher prototype was N165, which, unlike its two forebears, was built from the start as an amphibian (although the Flycatcher was designed to be easily converted from landplane to seaplane, and frequently was when in service). The amphibian version utilised much of the landplane undercarriage, including the oleo-pneumatic struts, but gained two wooden boat-built floats with wheels set in the planing bottoms. Flycatcher N165 is seen here taking off in 1926, some time before duralumin floats of a more modern design replaced the wooden ones. (Author's collection)

the upper and lower limits. (The Plover, which also had full span 'flaperons', could only position its flaps on two pre-set angles). The ailerons also had differential built into the circuit, meaning the 'down' aileron moved less, counteracting 'adverse yaw' (the tendency of an aircraft to turn against the direction of roll due to greater drag from the 'down' aileron).

The elevator was also rigged with a form of 'differential' movement, to provide greater travel the further it was deflected, with smaller movements and lower gearing at the centre. The variable-incidence tailplane was adjustable for trim using a wheel mounted on the starboard wall of the cockpit, and the rudder had a bias control to allow for airscrew torque.

The undercarriage was an exceptionally long-stroke arrangement based around a forward V-frame, which supported a trailing arm on each side each damped by a long travel oleo leg. The geometry was designed to enhance stability during the take-off and landing roll, and was as effective as it was inelegant.[3] The wheels could be exchanged for floats in a straightforward manner — a larger fin and rudder was fitted when the Flycatcher was configured as a floatplane, and this was also designed to be easily exchanged.

The first of the three prototype Flycatchers, N163, first flew at Hamble in November 1922 (around six months after the first Plover) and was delivered to the Aeroplane Evaluation Establishment at Martlesham Heath for performance trials early in 1923. These trials were extensive and thorough and included all aspects of flying handling and performance, stability, controllability, armament and engine. The engine fitted to N163 was an Armstrong Siddeley Jaguar III, but Fairey also had plans to fit a Bristol Jupiter, as had been fitted to the first Plover.

The pilots at Martlesham reported very favourably on the Flycatcher. Flight Lieutenant Orlebar noted that "no trouble has been experienced with construction (over 30 hours hard flying) which is of a high order". He

3. Fairey, J.S., Flycatcher Facsimile (part 1), Aeroplane Monthly March 1982 p.132.

One of the first two Parnall Plovers, in this case fitted with the two-row Armstrong-Siddeley Jaguar engine. The ungainly nature of the deep fuselage is clearly in evidence, although more attention has been paid to fairing the engine and the guns, which were concealed beneath the upper nose decking, than in the case of the Flycatcher. (Author's collection)

concluded that "the type has many excellent features as a deck landing scout," highlighting the pilot's view, the efficiency of the camber-changing gear, controllability at low speeds and the slow landing speed. Flight Lieutenant Fletcher, a pilot detached from HMS *Argus*, added "the stability of the aircraft is very good and is neither too light nor too heavy on controls. There appears to be no dangerous peculiarities and I consider the majority of pilots will have no difficulty in flying the type… The view from the pilot's seat is the best I have experienced for deck landing."[4]

In March 1923, both the Flycatcher and Plover prototypes took part in carrier-flying trials on HMS *Argus*. With basic service trials out of the way, the RN concentrated on intensive comparative testing between the two types. Once again, the Flycatcher drew praise for its performance, handling and practicality. One pilot noted simply "I have tested the machine in every way but can find no vices".[5]

The first Plover, N160, on the other hand appeared to be struggling, with pilots complaining of stiff controls, poor undercarriage design and inadequate control with the flaps extended. There were also worries about the view for air fighting and the aircraft's construction.

Fletcher, who had already flown the Flycatcher at Martlesham, said "Taking everything into consideration, there appears to be no doubt that the 'Flycatcher' is easily the better machine." Fairey's careful design was paying dividends and the Flycatcher was unanimously felt to have excellent deck-landing properties.

During the trials, Fairey received an order for a further three prototypes – Parnall had already received a similar order, in January, and the RN had still not committed to a type to equip its new Fleet Fighter Flights. Part of the

4. Trials of Fleet Fighters Flycatcher and Plover, Air 5/240, National Archives
5. Trials of Fleet Fighters Flycatcher and Plover, Air 5/240, National Archives.

The Parnall Plover, seen here in the redesigned form debuted from the third prototype, and rigged as an amphibian. The revised Plover design had a slightly better performance than the Flycatcher, and the Air Ministry's preferred engine, the nine-cylinder Bristol Jupiter. However, its construction was not as strong or durable as the Flycatcher's. (Author's collection)

reason for the drawn-out process was the number of tasks the aircraft would be required to undertake. With basic flying and deck-landing trials conducted, both fighters still had to be evaluated for flying off platforms mounted on battleships and cruisers, requiring even shorter take-off than on an aircraft carrier.

Furthermore installations of both engine types also had to be assessed. Despite the fact that a great deal of testing still to be done, the Flycatcher was deemed ready to enter limited service for front-line evaluation, and 402 Flight was formed in April 1923 – optimistically, as it turned out, and the Flight would have to wait for its aircraft.

In May the Air Staff expressed concerns that Fairey was not producing the aircraft quickly enough, and bemoaned the fact that the first six Flycatchers would not be available until the end of the following month. Even this would turn out to be wildly optimistic, not helped by the fact that Fairey was very busy at this time producing IIID reconnaissance aircraft for the RN, Australia and Portugal and the Fawn bomber for the RAF. (In fact, the six aircraft, made up of the first three Flycatcher prototypes and the three pre-production machines ordered in March, would not all be in the Royal Navy's hands until August 1924). The situation had become so parlous that the Admiralty began to take steps to have Sopwith Snipe fighters modified with Nightjar oleo undercarriage units to act as an interim ship fighter.[6] In fact, the second prototype, N164, did not fly for the first time until 5 May. The aircraft, fitted with a Jaguar engine, was flown by Vincent Nicholl, and went to the Aeroplane Experimental Establishment at Martlesham Heath just three days later.

6. Correspondence between CAS and AMSR 4 May 1923, in Trials of Fleet Fighters Flycatcher and Plover, Air 5/240, National Archives.

Flycatcher N9662 was tested at the A&AEE in January 1924, and then passed to 402 Flight, part of HMS Eagle's *air group, where the aircraft received the code '5'. In this photograph, taken in 1924, N9662 shows a configuration typical of early Flycatchers, with the propeller spinner fitted and one-piece, curved windscreen. (Author's collection)*

A further blow to Fairey arrived in June when it became apparent that Parnall had substantially redesigned the Plover after the first two prototypes had been built, and the third and all subsequent aircraft were built to a greatly improved design. The fuselage had been redesigned, and was now less deep and ungainly. The wings had a little more stagger. The redesign had given the aircraft a slightly lower angle of attack on the deck and had increased the gap between the cockpit and the upper wing; both changes served to improve the pilot's forward and downward view significantly.

Moreover, while Fairey had concentrated on the Jaguar installation, Parnall had done most work on fitting the Plover with the Jupiter, which it was becoming clear was the more powerful engine and preferred in some circles of the RN and Air Ministry.

Nevertheless, as trials continued through summer 1923, the favourable reports into the Flycatcher's performance led to small production orders. An order for six Flycatchers with Jaguar engines was placed in May, followed by a similar order for 26 machines in July. Some of the six available Plovers, meanwhile, went into front line service in June alongside Nightjars at 403 Flight aboard *Hermes* and 404 Flight aboard HMS *Furious*.

The third Flycatcher, N165, took to the air around August 1923. It appears to have been delayed by being built from the beginning in amphibian configuration, with wooden boat-type floats that had wheels set into the planing bottoms. It went to Gosport in September, followed by deck-landing trials in its amphibian configuration on HMS *Argus* in October.

The comparative trials between the two rival types continued into 1924. Further tests on the Flycatcher with the standard (360 hp) Jaguar were conducted at Northolt in January with RN pilots, and was passed fit for service. More Flycatchers began to join Fleet Fighter Flights in January 1924. Over the next six months, the

An Air Ministry photograph of an unusually bare Flycatcher, N9564, which only carried its serial in small letters on the rear fuselage and no fuselage roundel, unit markings or rudder serial. For reasons unknown, the tail fin has been retouched, although other photographs of this aircraft show no markings on the fin of any kind. In this image, the recessed wheels of the amphibian layout are very clear, as is the reuse of much of the landplane undercarriage hardware. (Author's collection)

experiences of those frontline units added to the findings of the ongoing trials. Nevertheless, the Fairey fighter had not yet won out. In production terms, Parnall received an order for 12 more Plovers in January 1924.

Flycatchers with 400 hp Bristol Jupiter and an uprated Jaguar offering 385 hp underwent service testing at Northolt when they became available, alongside Plovers. During these tests it was clear that the Plover had taken a significant leap forward and was in many respects now superior to the Flycatcher that had already been tested. Pilots found that with the same powerplant, the Plover was "appreciably faster"[7], lighter on the controls, nicer to fly and its gun installation was felt to be much better.

On the latter point, the service pilots might have been forgiven for thinking that Fairey had completely forgotten about the need to carry guns when designing the Flycatcher in contrast to the careful design throughout the rest of the aircraft. The two Vickers 0.303in machine guns were simply attached to adjustable brackets, in the open on each fuselage side, with no attempts at fairing or enclosing – the pilot had to lean out of the cockpit into the slipstream to reach the cocking lever. The Plover, meanwhile, carried its guns beneath the nose decking and the handles fell easily to hand within the cockpit.

Deck-landing difficulties

In June 1924, more comparative deck landing took place on *Argus*, this time with the newer Plover design and a Flycatcher fitted with a Bristol Jupiter. Both types proved far from ideal – Plover N9698 carried out several

7. Trials of Fleet Fighters Flycatcher and Plover, Air 5/240, National Archives.

Another view of the almost-unmarked N9664 rigged as an amphibian. The larger fin and rudder fitted to floatplane variants is apparent. The spray whipped up by the airscrew suggests the aircraft is at full power, preparing for take-off (which could be difficult unless there was enough chop to 'unstick' the floats). This Flycatcher went to RAF Kalafrana on Malta in unmarked condition in early 1925, as seen here, and later served with 402 Flight aboard HMS Eagle. *(ARCHIVE Images, www.archive-images.co.uk)*

landings but the general landing performance was poor and on the second day the Plover crashed over the side and was lost.

The Flycatcher fared no better, mainly because the centre-of-gravity of the Jupiter-engined machine N163 was too far forward. Fairey had modified the undercarriage to at least mitigate the increased possibility of nose-overs, but had not had time to redesign the fuselage and engine mount to bring the weight further aft.

Although take-off with the more powerful Jupiter proved shorter than the Jaguar-equipped aircraft, the altered balance made landings faster and longer. Indeed, on the first attempted deck landing with the Flycatcher, Flight Lieutenant Jones crashed on deck, wrecking the undercarriage and damaging the engine and fuselage.

For his own part, Jones' crash did not change his positive views of the Flycatcher. He admitted "I landed too fast and the machine ran to end of ramps and turned over on its nose. I attach no blame to the construction of the machine, and find it easy to handle in the air, has a good view and plenty of power."[8]

Nevertheless, the crash curtailed the tests, while concerns about the suitability of both aircraft for flying off battleship and cruiser platforms necessitated yet more trials to take place on *Argus* in July. A 17ft platform was fitted to the after end of the carrier's flight deck to replicate the flying-off platforms fitted to cruisers and battleships.

In 1917 and 1918, the Royal Naval Air Service (and later the RAF) had developed means of flying scout and reconnaissance aircraft from warships at sea. This was achieved by means of platforms placed on top of battleship turrets. The turrets could be swung so the ship did not even need to steam directly into the wind for the platform to be correctly aligned. A lengthways trestle carried the aircraft's tailskid, maintaining the aircraft at the correct attitude. The engine was run up while the aircraft was restrained, and then when it was released

8. Report on the deck landing trials of 'Fairey Flycatcher' by Flying Officer W. Jones, in Trials of Fleet Fighters Flycatcher and Plover, Air 5/240, National Archives.

the aeroplane would reach flying speed by the end of the platform. Light cruiser turrets were too small, but a purpose-built rotating platform for launching was fitted to more than 30 light cruisers.

This method was similar to that used by seaplane carriers, some of which had a short flying-off deck fitted. Seaplanes could therefore be launched using a wheeled trolley without the time-consuming need for lowering them over the side by crane.

These methods were, by the early 1920s, at risk from the general advancement of military aircraft which were quickly becoming larger and heavier. Though the Flycatcher is today considered a small and lightly-loaded aircraft, its full service weight was more than double that of the Sopwith Pup, which had been the first type in widespread use from turret platforms.

A number of take-offs and landings were carried out and it was concluded that both the Flycatcher and the Plover powered by the Jupiter would be able to operate from battleships with 20 knots of wind over the deck, and from cruisers with 28 knots of wind. There was insufficient margin of safety with the standard Jaguar III-powered Flycatcher.

By now, the need to conclude the protracted trial period was putting pressure on the RN. It was noted that the platform trials continued through difficult weather and conditions that "put a considerable strain on the endurance of the pilots taking part, particularly when launchings had to be repeated by the same pilots at short intervals".

Although it was not the main purpose of this sequence of trials, the landing performance of the Jupiter powered Flycatcher gave further cause for concern. The Flycatcher took almost twice as long to come to rest as the Plover did, and suffered several broken propellers, a damaged engine and a collapsed undercarriage. Even with ballast in the rear fuselage, the Flycatcher's centre of gravity was too far forward, which led to the landing speed being around 5 kt faster than that of the Plover.

The unusual sight of an amphibian Flycatcher fitted with the landplane tail. This aircraft, N9619, took part in the comparative tests with Parnall Plover prototypes aboard HMS Argus, *and later went to the Aeroplane and Armament Experimental Establishment, and then the Marine Aircraft Experimental Establishment, in November 1924, where it is seen here. In 1927, the aircraft was fitted with duralumin floats and took part in experiments to see whether floatplanes could land and take off from an aircraft carrier deck without any form of wheeled undercarriage (see 'Metal Floats and Airscrews', Chapter 4) (Author's collection)*

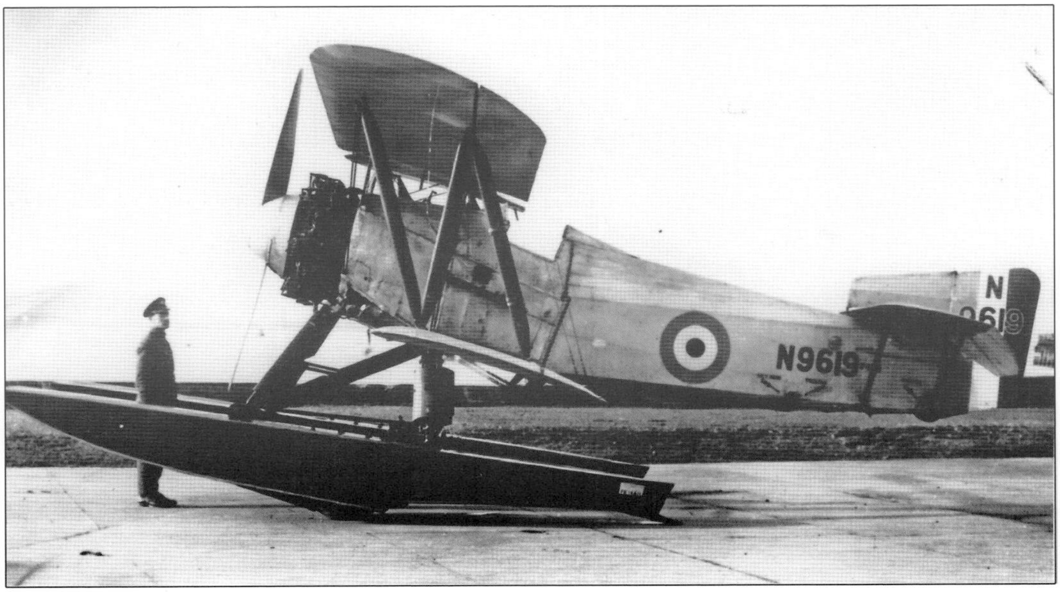

"I carried out launching and landing tests on this type last year," wrote Flight Lieutenant Fletcher, "and in my report stated that the machine was far too nose heavy for deck landing, and even showed a tendency to turn on its nose whilst taxiing at slow speed across an aerodrome. This nose heaviness I understand was due to the engine being installed too far forward and I submitted that either the engine should be set back, or the undercarriage put forward.

"The undercarriage has now been put forward but on flying this machine aboard for these trials I still found the machine nose heavy (in spite of carrying 28 lb weight in the aftermost bay of the fuselage)."[9]

The Admiralty and the Air Ministry were now in something of a dilemma. The improved Plover, powered by the favoured, more powerful Jupiter engine, had a significantly better performance than the standard Flycatcher. Its deck-landing difficulties had been fully rectified and it was now suitable for operation on aircraft carriers, battleships and cruisers.

Importantly, though, the construction, structural strength and longevity, of the Plover were in doubt. In July 1924, Plover N9704 of 405 Flight crashed in the river Eden when its upper wing centre-section partially collapsed, and less serious but still worrying structural issues had come to light during the ongoing trials.

A conference on the situation regarding the Flycatcher and Plover was held on 1 August 1924.[10] At the August 1924 meeting, the Air Staff, RAF, RN and Admiralty thrashed out the arguments. The Flycatcher, it was felt, had proved itself to be perfectly robust during limited operational service, and its handling and performance although slightly inferior to the improved Plover, were still found praiseworthy by pilots in their own right. The Flycatcher was, however, felt to be unsuitable for cruisers and battleship flying with the standard Jaguar III engine, and the preferred Jupiter degraded the Flycatcher's fine deck landing characteristics and its general suitability. The RN did not want to introduce two types into service, so would have to settle on one of them.

In the Plover's favour was its out-and-out performance, added to which were fears that Parnall might "go under" if the firm did not receive the order for the ship fighter[11]. Fairey, on the other hand, was not short of work – in fact it was full up to the extent of deliveries being sluggish.[12] Furthermore the Flycatcher had proved its robustness, and this was its chief advantage over the Plover. The representatives considered replacing the Flycatchers in service with Plovers, or retaining the existing Flycatchers alongside a smaller number of Plovers which would be used exclusively for flying off ship platforms.

This latter suggestion seemed to be a non-starter, as the CAS had declared in June 1924 that "The Air Staff Policy is that for types of which comparatively few [aircraft] will be required, such as Fleet Fighters, Fleet Spotters, Army Co-operation Aeroplanes, only one type of aeroplane and engine is to be used in the service."[13]

Fears about the Plover's structural weakness proved hard to overcome. The Chief of the Air Staff noted widespread fears that the Plover "would not stand the strain imposed upon it" and later that he "frankly would not trust to the Plover".[14] Nevertheless, it was considered that for the Flycatcher to use the Jupiter, it would have to be completely redesigned, and there was no guarantee that the redesign would be successful.

As it turned out, the factor that did most to tip the balance finally in favour of the Flycatcher was the availability of the improved Jaguar powerplant. Armstrong Siddeley had increased the available power from 325 hp

9. Report of pilot on launching and landing trials of Flycatcher (Jupiter) and Flycatcher (Boosted Jaguar), in Trials of Fleet Fighters Flycatcher and Plover, Air 5/240, National Archives.

10. Ibid.

11. Conference into Plover and Flycatcher, 1 August 1924, in Trials of Fleet Fighters Flycatcher and Plover, Air 5/240, National Archives.

12. Minutes of a conference held in CAS's room Air Ministry on Friday, 25 July 1924, at 11am, in Trials of Fleet Fighters Flycatcher and Plover, Air 5/240, National Archives.

13. New Types of Aeroplane, 12 June 1924, in Trials of Fleet Fighters Flycatcher and Plover, Air 5/240, National Archives.

14. Conference into Plover and Flycatcher, 1 August 1924, in Trials of Fleet Fighters Flycatcher and Plover, Air 5/240, National Archives.

This Flycatcher, N9678, was the first production amphibian. It underwent testing at the Marine Aircraft Experimental Establishment at Felixstowe in Suffolk in early 1924 and the seaplane tender HMS Pegasus *in March that year, before operating from the cruisers HMS* Enterprise *and HMS* Caledon *in 1926. (Author's collection)*

to 360 hp and then to 385 hp, with a variant that would become the Jaguar IV. This engine put the sparkle back into Fairey's fighter, and gave it the final edge during the discussions over which ship fighter to order.

It was a gamble on the part of the Air Staff and Admiralty, as the improved Jaguar was unproven at the time of the August 1924 conference. It nearly wasn't considered at all; during the later trials aboard *Argus*, the officer in charge of the programme sanctioned the inclusion of a 385 hp Jaguar-powered Flycatcher, even though the Air Staff and Admiralty had asked for trials only on the Jupiter-powered machines, and the Armstrong-Siddeley engine had not yet passed its type tests, so this was a lucky break for Fairey. The experiences here, and earlier in the year at Northolt, persuaded most of the service pilots that, overall, the Flycatcher was the better bet. It had a performance that was, in most regimes, equal to or only slightly poorer than that of the Plover, but with the benefit of much greater robustness and practicality.

In August, the 385 hp Jaguar IV passed its service tests and the decision was therefore made that the Flycatcher with this engine would be the Fleet Air Arm's main fighter "definitely until 1926". (Ironically, one factor in the decision not to proceed with the Plover was the feeling that a substantially better aircraft would be available in a few years and in those circumstances it was not worth changing from the Flycatcher).[15] In fact, during the Flycatcher's service, the Jaguar was developed into the MkIVC which could develop 400 hp in normal circumstances and 447 hp in an emergency, and many aircraft were fitted with this variant. The Jaguar IVC passed its type tests on 22 October 1929.

Orders for over 100 further Flycatchers were placed in 1924, and subsequent orders brought the total number of Flycatchers, including prototypes, to 193.

15. 'In two years time or so we may evolve something really much better, which would be worth changing over for' – CAS quoted in minutes of conference into Plover and Flycatcher, 1 August 1924, Air 5/240.

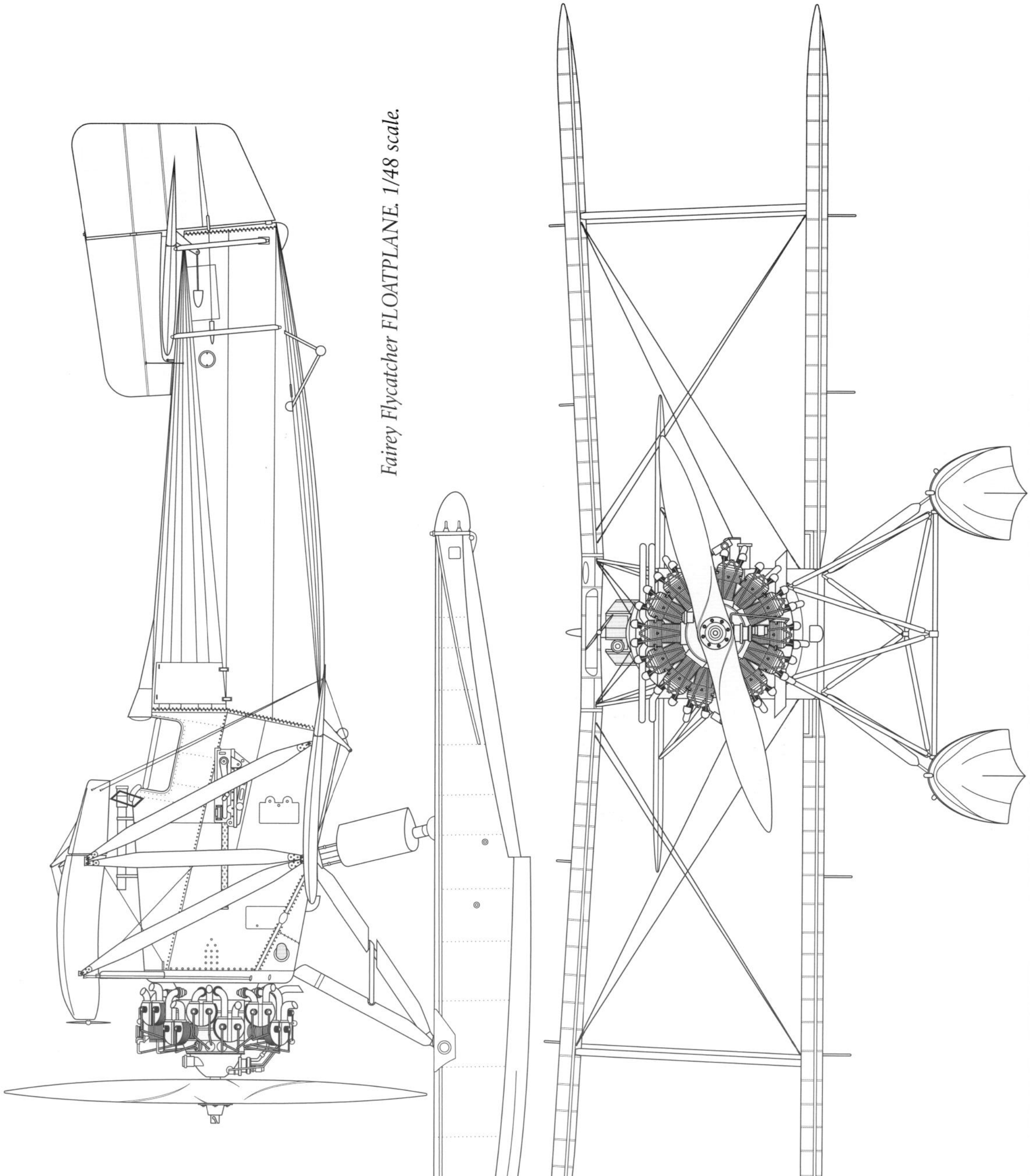

Fairey Flycatcher FLOATPLANE. 1/48 scale.

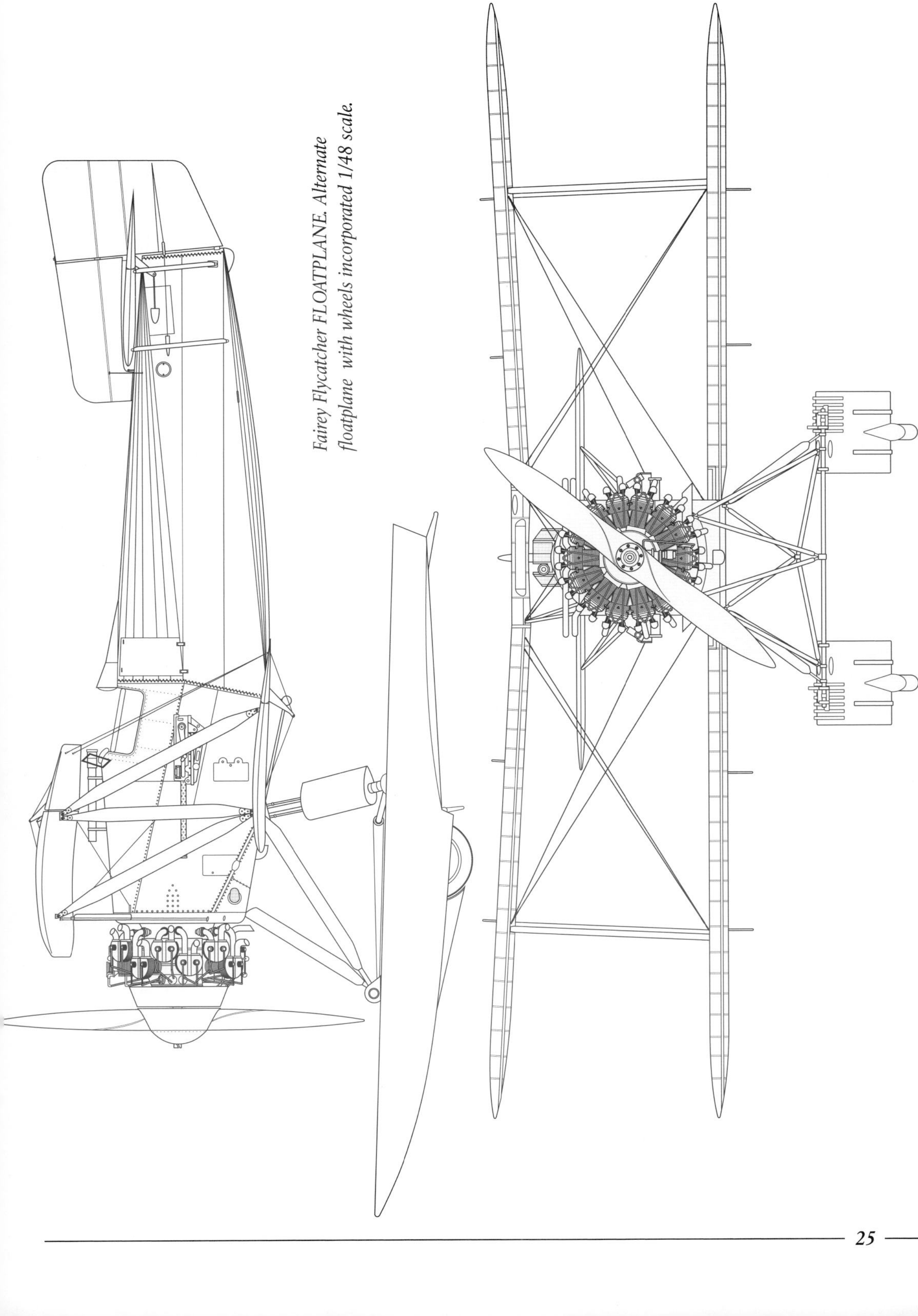

Fairey Flycatcher FLOATPLANE. Alternate floatplane with wheels incorporated 1/48 scale.

Development did not stop here, however. Numerous further tests and trials took place with the Flycatcher over the succeeding decade. These included the usual variety of experiments and assessments. In October 1924, for example, Flycatcher N9616 was trialled with a variety of airscrews by the Aeroplane and Armament Experimental Establishment, Martlesham Heath. The airscrews were the standard units as fitted to the Gloster Grebe and two types fitted to the Armstrong Whitworth Siskin, both types which also used the Jaguar engine.[16] The aim was to assess if any significant increase in climb performance could be obtained by this simple measure. The results showed that the existing Flycatcher airscrew was more or less the best for the aircraft, matched by one of the Siskin units.

As well as tests to develop the aircraft, Flycatchers were engaged throughout their career in trials and experiments aimed at developing the Fleet Air Arm's systems and practices. This included trials with the embryonic catapults and accelerators, different designs of float and bombing the radio-controlled target battleship HMS *Centurion*. (See Chapter 4 'Advancing the State of the Art')

16. Flight Tests of various airscrews in Fairey Flycatcher with Jaguar IV engine, under AVIA 18/1525.

The Flycatcher in service

The Fairey Flycatcher entered service gradually, during the lengthy period of trials and evaluation intended to settle which aircraft would equip the Fighter Flights of the Fleet Air Arm (FAA). 'Flights' were the unit of aircraft used by the Fleet Air Arm from 1923 to 1933, and usually comprised six aircraft. The Flights were initially arranged into four categories– Fleet Fighter, Fleet Spotter, Fleet Reconnaissance and Fleet Torpedo. Number 402 Flight was the first dedicated Flycatcher unit to be established, in April 1923, but it did not have a full complement of aircraft until rather later in the year. This Flight was assigned to HMS *Eagle*'s air group and its experiences fed into the ongoing trials.

When it was finally decided that the Flycatcher, and not the Parnall Plover, would be the main Fleet Air Arm fighter, all the existing Fleet Fighter Flights steadily began to replace their Plovers and Nieuport Nightjars with the Fairey aircraft. This took place between February 1924 and March 1925 when 404 Flight exchanged its Plovers, while 406 Flight was formed from scratch on Flycatchers in May 1924. Two further Fighter Flights, 407 and 408, were subsequently formed with Flycatchers in 1927 and 1929. The remaining Plovers were used for training.

A batch of 26 Flycatchers (N9655 to N9680), to be fitted with the '390 hp Jaguar', was ordered on 19 July 1923. This was followed by an order for 42 aircraft (N9854 to N9895) and a further order for 64 (N9902 to N9965) in 1924. A further 14 were ordered in 1925 (S1060 to S1073), 25 in 1928 (S1273 to S1297, minus S1284 which was released for evaluation in Argentina), 10 in 1930 (S1409 to S1418). A final order for a single aircraft, numbered S1590, actually represented the machine that had gone to Argentina and been returned.[1]

Training the Fighter Flights

The Royal Navy's (RN) training stations at Leuchars and Gosport began to receive Flycatchers throughout 1924 and 1925 to prepare new pilots for squadron service. The aircraft made a good impression on the new, peacetime intake as Owen Cathcart-Jones later wrote in his 'Aviation Memoirs':

1. Sturtivant, R. and Cronin, D., Fleet Air Arm Aircraft, Units and Ships 1920 to 1939, pp. 170-176.

Flycatcher N9915 was relatively unusual in spending all of its career with the same establishment, in this case, RAF Leuchars. This was one of the main shore training stations for Flycatchers, and which enabled floatplane training on the Tay - N9915 was operated as a floatplane with 'A' Training Flight, and later as a landplane with 'B' Flight. It is seen here above the Scottish countryside. (Author's collection)

"We were then flying Fleet Fighters in the shape of Fairey Flycatchers, really remarkable machines, of exceptional strength and an amazing performance combining fairly high top speed with a very slow landing speed, which was exactly what was required for deck landing on a carrier... They were ideal machines for aerobatics and strong enough to resist the terrific strains which were subsequently imposed upon them in our endeavours to outdo each other in some particularly brilliant aerobatic."[2]

John Nesbitt-Dufort also trained on Flycatchers, and wrote in his book 'Open Cockpit' that "the flying characteristics were good and although lateral control could have been a shade lighter this neat little fighter was very manoeuvrable and could be turned on a postage-stamp."[3]

The training involved all the flying modes practiced by the Fleet Air Arm in this period. Dummy deck landing was rehearsed incessantly on a flight deck shape marked out on the aerodrome surface. This was done for hours at a time with the pilots making repeated left-hand circuits of the airfield waiting for the 'deck' control officer to signal them individually with an Aldis lamp to make their approach. Interestingly though, no deck-landing aboard a carrier was practised during basic training, and this had to wait until pilots were assigned to a Flight. Nevertheless, the business of deck landing was evidently taken very seriously – Cathcart-Jones reports that whenever pilots flew ashore from their carrier they would spend around two hours on dummy deck landings.[4]

2. Cathcart-Jones, Owen, Aviation Memoirs, Hutchinson & Co. 1934, p.57.
3. Nesbitt-Dufort, J., Open Cockpit: Flying Pre-War Fighting and Training Aircraft, Speed and Sports Publications 1970, p.32.
4. Cathcart-Jones, Owen, Aviation Memoirs, Hutchinson & Co. 1934, p.64.

Even at training establishments, Flycatchers quickly gained colourful and individualistic markings. This unidentified aircraft with unusual star markings on the wheel hubs is seen at RAF Leuchars in Fife, in front of the Belfast Truss hangars built in 1917-18. It also has a broad, dark band painted around the spinner. The mounting bracket for a Vickers machine gun is fitted, but no gun attached. Leuchars was one of the main land bases for Fleet Air Arm aircraft in the 1920s (Author's collection)

A pair of Flycatchers at a shore base. Flycatcher N9873, in the foreground, was delivered to 401 Flight at RNAS Donibristle in December 1925. Here is it most likely at a training establishment, as it appears to have a single code letter with serif of the kind seen on Flycatchers based at Leuchars. (Author's collection)

The training programme also included flying from platforms of the sort fitted to battleships and cruisers, as this was still an important part of the Fleet Air Arm's role until catapults gained dominance. A mock-up of the platform was set up at each of the training aerodromes with a tail trestle and quick-release apparatus to mimic the system aboard ships – although the mock-up could not replicate the headwind of 20 kt or more which enabled take-off in the space of a few yards.

Training also included floatplane flying, and for much of the Flycatcher's service, this meant aircraft equipped with wooden, flat-bottomed floats. These were not always fully effective and if conditions were calm, it could be very difficult to 'unstick' the floats from the water. Crews based at Leuchars conducted floatplane training on the Tay, and it was relatively common for aircraft to be seen running up and down repeatedly before they could get into the air, especially if conditions were too calm. Unfortunately, if conditions were too rough, it was possible for the Flycatcher to start pitching and break the wooden propeller on a wave.

Later, Flycatchers were fitted with Fairey-Reed propellers, which were formed from a solid 'plank' of duralumin and twisted to shape, which had been trialled on N165 at Felixstowe in April 1926. The development of duralumin 'V'-bottom floats also helped to solve many of the floatplane take-off problems. The third prototype, N165 first tested these in June 1926, although the wooden floats remained in use in some cases until relatively late until the Flycatcher's career (See chapter 4).

During work-up with operational Flights, methods of using the Flycatcher in action were developed. The aircraft would not just be used as fighters but for diversionary and flak-suppression attacks while escorting strike aircraft, and sometimes to make attacks in their own right. The methods devised were described by Cathcart-Jones:

A Flycatcher stunts above RAF Leuchars, where much of the training of operational Flycatcher pilots took place. Accounts such as Owen Cathcart-Jones' 'Aviation Memoirs' reveal that students had a great deal of fun flying the manoeuvrable and responsive biplane around the Fife landscape. (Fleet Air Arm Museum)

Flycatchers N9865 and N9855 at RAF Gosport, where Flycatchers were employed training frontline pilots, and were also repaired and reconditioned. These two aircraft carry no Fleet Fighter Flight markings, though both equipped frontline units at various times. N9865 went to Gosport for repair after an accident with 404 Flight aboard HMS Furious *in September 1925, while N9855 was badly damaged as a result of going over the side of the same carrier in January 1926. It is likely that both aircraft are seen here after repair. (Andy Pym collection)*

A different angle of the same two aircraft, N9865 and N9855 (Andy Pym collection)

"Our original method of bombing was to take up a position at about 2,000 ft immediately above the target, pull the nose up into a gradual stall and let the machine drop in a vertical dive on to the target. While in the dive we aligned our sights on the target and released the bomb."

A method of attacking ground targets that has been closely associated with the Flycatcher's time in service was developed around this time, which Cathcart-Jones described:

"Shortly after this a new and far more accurate method of bombing was introduced. It was known as converging bombing... during converging bombing we split up and took up positions round the target equidistant from each other. The leader would signal by rocking his wings and then commence the exercise by diving at the target. When he was nearing the base of his dive, No.2 would start from another direction, followed by No.3 from the opposite side. By the time No.3 was finishing his dive, No.1 had already got into position again and commenced his second dive, with the result that there was always one machine diving at the target."[5]

'Youthful High Spirits'

The trainee pilots worked hard, but also played hard. The Flycatcher's strength and aerobatic ability led pilots to push the boundaries of what was possible. Pilots taking part in Leuchars courses were eventually forbidden from flying near the Tay Bridge, after railway officials complained that Flycatchers had been seen flying beneath the spans of the structure. Other 'high-jinks' during training included flying alongside express trains and waving to the passengers, taking whole formations through the narrowest valleys, and 'buzzing'

5. Cathcart-Jones, Owen, Aviation Memoirs, Hutchinson & Co. 1934, p.64.

Flycatcher N9669, bearing three signal pennants on her tail fin that, read downwards, read '4-0-5', suggesting that it was taken during the aircraft's spell with 405 Flight between September 1924 and April 1925. It then served in 'A' (Fighter) Training Flight at RAF Leuchars in 1925 and early 1926. Vickers guns are fitted. (Andy Pym collection)

guest houses popular with visiting relatives of Fleet Air Arm personnel. In fact this expression of high spirits continued into front-line service, and over the course of the Flycatcher's career a number of aircraft and even some pilots were lost due to crashes resulting from low level aerobatics.

The Flycatcher's aerobatic ability was not lost on the FAA's more official circles. 'Flying the Flag' around the Empire and other nations was an important part of the RN's duties during the 1920s and 1930s, and the Flycatcher was the ideal tool for demonstrating the Navy's prowess. Demonstrations of formation and aerobatic flying took place frequently. These included the resident China Station Flight celebrating the King's birthday with a massed formation flyover of Happy Valley (which also helped serve as a helpful 'show of force' in the face of unrest in the region). Displays were sometimes staged to salute carriers' captains at the end of a commission. Flycatchers also made contributions to air pageants at Malta and at home. One-off displays were also carried out, such as an individual aerobatic display in a floatplane Flycatcher to entertain the crowds before the 1929 Schneider Trophy race, and a formation and aerobatic presentation to Greek flying officers during a cruise in the Aegean.

Even the standard 'break to land' procedure of 404 Flight during its time with HMS *Courageous* reads like a set-piece of the Red Arrows. Owen Cathcart-Jones recalled: "we did our usual 'Flight break up' of a dive; and as we pulled up, the leader would do the first half of a loop, then roll off his back; the two on each side of him a complete loop, and the two outside pilots a stall-turn, while the one 'in the box' – which was myself – would fly straight on."

Take-offs and landings

Flycatchers were stationed on a number of capital ships and cruisers, individually and in small detachments. Nine capital ships operated Flycatchers from turret ramps between 1924 and 1931. In addition, at least three light cruisers operated Flycatchers from revolving platforms – HMS *Caledon* carried Flycatchers including N9679

Flycatcher N9673 of 401 Flight at RAF Cranwell, site of the RAF College, in 1929. (Author's collection)

The Flycatcher was developed not just to operate from aircraft carriers but from cruisers and battleships as well. Light cruisers such as HMS Enterprise, *seen here in 1930 on service in the East Indies, carried a Flycatcher on a rotating platform amidships – floatplane N9965 can be seen here on its platform, just ahead of the after mast, which could be rotated into the apparent wind to allow take-off without the ship having to alter course. The Flycatcher would take off like a landplane using a wheeled trolley. (Author's collection)*

and N9902 during its time with the Atlantic and Mediterranean Fleets, HMS *Enterprise* and HMS *Emerald* carried a Flycatcher each while serving on the East Indies station, and heavy cruisers sometimes operated Flycatchers as well.

Some of these ships flew the Flycatchers directly off the platform as landplanes, while in other instances they were rigged as floatplanes and merely stored on the platform to be craned over the side when required.

The process of flying off a turret platform was described by former Flycatcher pilot John Nesbitt-Dufort DSO in 'Open Cockpit': "a small platform was built over the 12 in guns of a capital ship and the Flycatcher was mounted actually on the platform over the gun turret with skid up in an elevated trough in which there was a small release catch. The battleship was steamed at full speed and the gun turret swung into the resulting wind, the 'Catcher's

HMS Enterprise *during her time with the 4th Cruiser Squadron on the East Indies station in the early 1930s. The wings and tail of her Flycatcher, N9965, can be seen aft of the second funnel, mounted on the rotating launch platform. She was later fitted with a catapult and the Flycatcher was replaced by a Hawker Osprey. (Author's collection)*

A photograph of Fairey Flycatcher floatplane N9965 taken from the parent ship HMS Enterprise *around 1930 during one of several periods of duty the ship spent on the East Indies station between 1928 and 1936. Flycatcher N9965 was the last aircraft to be built in the third and largest production batch. Before being assigned to* Enterprise, *N9965 spent time with 404 Flight aboard HMS* Furious *and 401 Flight aboard HMS* Hermes. *(Author's collection)*

In addition to cruisers, Flycatchers were assigned to battleships and battle cruisers. Unlike the cruisers, which needed a purpose-built turntable, the larger ships could fit a launching platform above a gun turret, using the turret itself to swing the aircraft into the wind. Here, the battle cruiser HMS Repulse *carries a Flycatcher, rigged as a landplane, on her 'Y' turret platform. The platforms were generally phased out in favour of catapults towards the end of the 1920s. (Author's collection)*

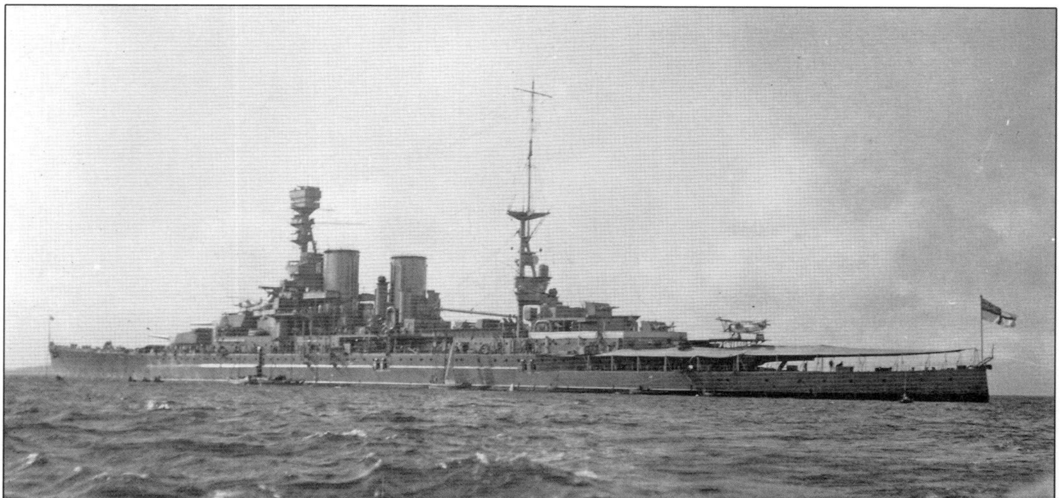

A Flycatcher, probably S1280 of 406 Flight, about to launch from the 'B' Turret ramp on the battleship HMS Ramillies, *of the 1st Battle Squadron, in 1931. Flycatchers were developed not just for service with Fleet Fighter units operating from aircraft carriers, but also from battleships and cruisers, carrying out defence and scouting duties. Before catapults were commonplace, the aircraft launched from platforms, effectively tiny flight decks, which could be angled into wind. (Fleet Air Arm Museum)*

A Flycatcher floatplane wearing an unusually dark colour, pulled up on a beach alongside three Fairey IIID floatplanes. The aircraft could be from the Seaplane Training Flight, Calshot, with which IIID S1035 '50' served with in 1929–30. (Author's collection)

engine was wound up to maximum revs and at the 'moment critique' someone pulled the plug, releasing the tail skid stop, and in about three seconds, all being well, the little fighter was airborne."[6]

The Flycatcher was versatile enough to serve as a landplane from aircraft with no flight deck, but the FAA also saw the benefits of operating the fighter as a floatplane from an aircraft carrier. HMS *Hermes* was operated as a pure seaplane carrier at times when on the China Station, when all her aircraft would be converted to floatplane undercarriage and the ship herself used as a mobile base. Wheel undercarriages were only refitted during these periods to help pilots maintain their deck-landing currency.

When the Flycatcher entered service, the deck-landing system of longitudinal wires was the favoured means of retaining aircraft on landing. As opposed to later systems of wires designed to slow aircraft down, the longitudinal wires were chiefly intended to stop a landing aeroplane drifting, overturning or worst of all, falling over the side of the deck. Deck-landing aircraft had jaws known as 'Bryer Hooks' fitted to the undercarriage to engage with wires, in theory preventing them from drifting or bouncing after touchdown. Some ships had other devices to gradually retard the landing roll. HMS *Argus*, for example, had hinged vertical flaps known as 'hurdles' which landing aircraft knocked flat as they ran along the deck.

The Flycatcher, unlike the Parnall Plover, had proved relatively well suited from the beginning for using the system of longitudinal wires. Nevertheless, it became clear over time that the wires were causing more accidents than they prevented. Numerous minor incidents led to damage to propellers, wingtips and undercarriages, but more seriously, an aircraft that made an imperfect landing but had hooked a wire had no chance to put the matter right by taking off again. This came to a head when a Fairey IIID pilot was killed after an attempted landing on HMS *Hermes*, tried to go round again but snagged a wire and fell over the side. It fell to Flycatcher pilot Lieutenant Owen Cathcart-Jones to assess the possibility of landing with no deck aids at all, the attempt to be made on 8 April 1926. He recalled:

"Bryan's death was not in vain. After his accident, it was decided to experiment with landing on the deck without the use of the wires, which had proved the cause of so many accidents in the past, and on 8 April I made two more deck landings on the *Hermes* without the use of any arresting wires stretched along the deck."

This proved that it was not only possible but preferable to land aboard a carrier without restraining the sideways movement of the landing aircraft, and that it was safer to allow a pilot to go around again if the first attempt failed.

Protecting shipping in China

Although Flycatchers never went to war in the strictest sense, they were at the forefront of the RN's response to heightened tensions around the British Empire and areas of British interest. This included the escalation of fighting between warlords in China, which broke into full civil war in 1927.

After the Qing Dynasty collapsed in 1911, China entered the so-called 'Warlord Era'. The overall government of the country broke down and much of Northern China was seized by a number of military rulers while the South (including the area adjacent to the British protectorate of Hong Kong) fell under the control of the Kuomintang party's nationalists.

The increasingly volatile situation in China threatened British interests including civilian shipping and Hong Kong. Anti-British feeling steadily increased over this period and led to a long-running boycott and strike, and theft of British cargo lighters in Hong Kong harbour by communist sympathisers. When Vice-Admiral Alexander-Sinclair took over command of the China Station in September 1925, he noted that the action had

6. Nesbitt-Dufort, J., Open Cockpit: Flying Pre-War Fighting and Training Aircraft, Speed and Sports Publications 1970, p.29.

HMS Hermes, *saluting the flag of the Commander in Chief as she departs Devonport after a refit, before picking up her aircraft at Spithead and departing for the China Station.* Hermes *initially served on the China Station in 1925, but was quickly withdrawn for modification to make her more suitable for operation in hot climates. She returned, carrying 403 Flight's Flycatchers, in 1926, in time to undertake 'colonial policing' and anti-piracy operations. (Author's collection)*

brought British coastal shipping to "a standstill" and local British trade was reduced to "very small proportions". Meanwhile, Soviet steamers arriving daily were suspected of bringing arms and ammunition.[7]

An American merchant ship was fired on from the coast, suffering over 200 small-arms hits and one artillery shell. Bombs in Thermos flasks were smuggled aboard British merchant ships on a number of occasions. In October 1925, one of these detonated on the SS *Tuckwo*, injuring two Chinese passengers. British armed launches were frequently fired upon. Alexander-Sinclair feared that an 'outrage' committed against Westerners was a serious risk at any time, and that this could draw the nations involved into war.

Furthermore, piracy had returned to Southern Chinese waters, in an up-to-date form. The new pirates have been compared with 'modern day hi-jackers':

"Disguised as passengers, they seized ships when they had just left Hong Kong near Bias Bay... The China Navigation Company vessel [SS *Anking*] was carrying over 1,000 passengers from Singapore to Amoy when it was hijacked by pirates who had boarded the ship in Singapore. They then redirected it to Bias Bay and looted the passengers."[8]

British forces were engaged to help stop the attacks, including detachments of soldiers from the Hong Kong garrison travelling aboard. These measures did not stop the attacks, however. It proved hard for the RN to deal with the menace, given the desperation with which the pirates sometimes acted. After the SS *Irene* was taken over, the submarines HMS L-4 and HMS L-5 could not dislodge the pirates and sank the ship. The pirates

7. China Station General Letter No,2 under ADM 1/8705/193, National Archives.
8. Kwong Chi Man and Tsoi Yi Lun, Eastern Fortress: A Military History of Hong Kong, 1840-1970, Hong King University Press 2014, p.79.

The Royal Navy's China Station, at Hong Kong Harbour between the wars. HMS Eagle *can be seen at the far right hand side, in the furthest row of ships.* Eagle *operated Flycatchers on the China Station in 1925 and 1926, during unrest and high levels of piracy. Also visible are numerous County-class heavy cruisers, a C-class light cruiser and several destroyers. (Author's collection)*

were apprehended but 28 passengers had died and a diplomatic incident (the ship was owned by the Chinese government), that was not resolved for many years, resulted.

The attempted capture of the SS *Sunning* in November 1926 was probably the best known example. Around forty pirates who had been posing as passengers took control of the ship, threatening the officers with death if they did not comply. However, after eight hours the crew and passengers attacked the pirates, retaking control of the vessel. The pirates set fire to the ship's upperworks in the hope of flushing the crew out of the bridge but, being unable to do so, elected to leave in the ship's boats. RN ships later captured all the pirates, but only by virtue of the passengers' and crew's courageous actions. In most cases the merchant ships were not so fortunate.

It was suspected, though could not be proven, that the piracy had the tacit approval of the local government, or senior figures within it, as Canton rarely acted on reports of such activity from the British. An estimated average of three British or other non-Chinese ships were seized every year during the 1920s, and many more ships sailing under the Chinese flag.[9]

It was into this situation that HMS *Hermes* arrived at Hong Kong, in August 1925, to reinforce the China Station in its efforts to deal with the increasing instability and threats to shipping. Aircraft from *Hermes* patrolled the frontier at the request of the Governor for three months, and the carrier made cruises up the coast as part of a visible British presence. The temporary airstrip established at Kowloon (later Kai Tak airport) in the mid-1920s enabled plenty of flying for 401 Flight's Flycatchers.

Unfortunately, it soon became obvious that *Hermes* needed modifications to make the vessel suitable for use in very hot climates, so her initial stay on the station was relatively short. The Commander in Chief of the China Station wanted to retain some of her aircraft, but as the Colonial Government had taken over the landing ground at Kowloon it was not clear whether it would continue to be available for Naval use.

The carrier left in February and returned to the Mediterranean, leaving HMS *Vindictive* to operate seaplanes in the region. *Vindictive* was a light cruiser adapted to carry aircraft, with a hangar and transverse compressed-air

9. Lilius, Aleko E., I Sailed With Chinese Pirates, Earnshaw Books 2009.

catapult replacing 'B' turret. (*Vindictive* was the first RN cruiser with a catapult, some time before they became standard). A detachment of Flycatcher floatplanes from 401 Flight accompanied Fairey IIID reconnaissance aircraft aboard. The vessel arrived at Hong Kong in February 1926, and cruised extensively around the Chinese coast with its aircraft over the next two years, supported at times by the addition of aircraft carriers.

Hermes returned to China at the end of 1926, based at Hong Kong, joined in early 1927 by *Argus*, which was stationed further north but was not carrying any fighters at this time. *Hermes*' air group decided that it would be best employed as a seaplane force, and all the 403 Flight Flycatchers were fitted with floats. This enabled the carrier to be used as a mobile base of operations, transporting seaplanes to various points along the coast where they would patrol and act as a 'show of force'. Owen Cathcart-Jones described the procedure used:

"Each Flycatcher was stowed in the hangar on board, its floats resting on a large mobile trolley... The machines were then brought up to the flying deck and arranged in a small semicircle beneath the travel of the crane's arm, ready to hoist us over the side in quick succession."

It was clear that the situation was becoming hotter. Fighting was fierce and Western interests were increasingly under threat. As well as the risk from the warring factions, the instability emboldened the pirates, who were operating from small villages in remote stretches of coast. This prompted 401 Flight to ramp up their operational preparations, and training took place with live ammunition and bombs. Air-to-air gunnery was practised with drogues towed by a Fairey IIID, and dive-bombing took place using a large rock protruding from the sea outside Hong Kong Harbour.

Two Flycatchers '8' and '4' of 403 Flight, HMS Hermes, *taxiing on floats off Wei Hei Wei in 1926, during the commission where HMS* Hermes' *Flycatchers operated almost exclusively as floatplanes. The Flight was employed patrolling for pirates and acting as a deterrent for parties acting against British interests. The Flight also took part in combined operations to flush out pirate ringleaders after a number of merchant ships were seized. (Fleet Air Arm Museum)*

When HMS Hermes *joined the China Station in 1926, the ship operated as a seaplane carrier with all its 403 Flight Flycatchers converted to floatplane configuration. This aircraft, N9908 '2', was fitted with floats on 14 June 1926. It was flown by Lieutenant G.F. Renwick when, during a landing in formation on 22 April the following year, N9908 began to drift and the port undercarriage struts collapsed. Renwick escaped without injury but his aircraft, seen here during its recovery, was less fortunate. (Author's collection)*

Matters came to a head after the SS *Sunning* incident. A combined operation was planned with Royal Marines and police storming the pirates' lair at Bias Bay with Flycatchers from *Hermes* providing support from the air.

"Our Flight was to go into immediate action, loaded up with bombs and live ammunition", recalled Owen Cathcart-Jones, "to carry out an anti-pirate patrol to Bias Bay in co-operation with a Naval landing force from the *Hermes* and the rest of the Fleet."

He added: "We were to circle round and round the village of Fan-lo-kong, at the base of Bias Bay, which was to be surrounded by the landing force, accompanied by the Hong Kong police, who had descriptions of all the most notorious pirates inhabiting this district.

"We were neither to take action nor open fire unless we observed bandits who had escaped through the cordon running away into fairly open country round the village," Cathcart-Jones added. The operation was a success – the pirate stronghold was destroyed, the leaders captured, and no-one braved the cordon of circling Flycatchers. This was the beginning of further success against the pirates – patrolling aircraft from *Hermes* were later able to locate pirates at sea and prevent their escape, which played a significant part in keeping the pirate menace from completely hamstringing shipping in the region, though piracy remained a problem until the Second World War.

Flycatchers of 403 Flight continued their association with HMS *Hermes*, but in January 1933, the establishment was increased to supply aircraft to the 5th Cruiser Squadron, which was made up of HMS *Berwick*, HMS *Cornwall*, HMS *Cumberland*, HMS *Kent* and HMS *Suffolk*. These aircraft were fitted with catapult spools and were all operating from the cruisers' catapults by March.

Flash points and flashy flying

HMS *Courageous*, together with HMS *Glorious* had been converted from fast, lightly armoured battle cruisers in similar fashion to their half-sister HMS *Furious*. In 1928, *Courageous* was commissioned and joined by Flycatchers from 404 and 407 Flights, to form part of the Mediterranean Fleet. The small size and specialist nature of the Fleet Air Arm had led to a great sense of professionalism and the new carriers were no exception. Owen Cathcart-Jones, having transferred to 404 Flight, recalled the pride in carrying out evolutions as smartly as possible shared by air crews and those on deck:

"Soon the men of our Flight caught the same fever for speed. They would pride themselves on the short time taken to open hangar doors, prepare aircraft, and start engines. All this training was of the utmost use once we were on board, and it was through our high speed efficiency that we were able to put up almost incredible records for getting a Flight of six fighters up from the hangar in *Courageous* on to the flying deck, take off and land again. On one occasion, we landed the whole six aircraft on the deck in four minutes thirty seconds, which I don't think has, or ever will be, beaten."[10]

The three converted battle cruisers had the unusual feature of a small flying-off deck separate from the main deck on the bow of the ship. This deck ran directly from the forward hangar where one flight of Flycatchers (HMS *Glorious* and *Courageous* operated two Fighter Flights unlike all previous carriers, which only operated one Flight) was customarily stored.[11]

From this position, the 'slip flight' Flycatchers could be wheeled to their flying-off position without needing to use the lifts. The engine would be run up to full throttle while a hydraulically-operated windbreak shielded the aircraft. The windbreak would then fold out of the way, the Flycatcher was released and would be airborne almost immediately. T.W. Fish of 462 Torpedo Flight recalled the procedure in a letter to Flight:

10. Cathcart-Jones, Owen, Aviation Memoirs, Hutchinson & Co. 1934, p.153.
11. HMS Glorious, Flight, 16 May 1930, p.540.

Flycatchers of 402 Flight, HMS Eagle, *c.1926-8 showing the unit's black fuselage chevrons and concentric wheel hub circles, and single-digit codes. The lower image shows three aircraft over the Mediterranean.*
(Upper image, author's collection; lower image, Fleet Air Arm Museum)

"The tail would rise to flying position while the aircraft was still tethered and, when released, the Flycatcher roared straight out over the forecastle flight deck and was airborne well before reaching the ship's bows."[12]

A series of photographs in Flight magazine from 16 May 1930 confirm this – one image shows the Flycatcher reaching the forward windbreak while rolling, and in the next, having just passed the windbreak, the Flycatcher has several feet of air beneath its wheels.

The slow landing speed and handiness of the Flycatcher helped prevent many accidents, even though the light weight and low wing-loading of type the meant it could be susceptible to gusty wind on landing. Before barriers were introduced during the Second World War, each aircraft had to be sent down to the hangar before the next could land. The Flycatcher was so light that the procedure was developed for a landing party to run out and steady the aircraft, catch it, and wheel it by hand to the lift. The Flight report on HMS *Glorious* in 1930 referred to "a Flycatcher which landed and then got caught in a gust and slewed towards the ship's side before the landing crew had time to catch it; it was then righted, wheeled forward to the lift and sent down."[13]

Readiness for combat

Though the Flycatcher never took part in air combat, the Fleet Fighter Flights worked their aircraft hard preparing their pilots and tactics for the day when they might be needed in earnest. Numerous fleet exercises were held, usually with at least one aircraft carrier on each side. The Flycatchers were responsible for escorting torpedo bombers, initially Blackburn Darts and subsequently Ripons, and for carrying out diversionary attacks on target ships with guns and small bombs. This foreshadowed the co-ordinated dive-bombing and torpedo attack that would be practised by most naval air arms until the end of the Second World War. Although a not entirely realistic experience, these exercises undoubtedly taught the pilots much about air combat.

One large exercise that involved multiple Flights of Flycatchers as well as other elements of the Fleet Air Arm and surface fleet was Exercise NY, carried out in the Mediterranean on 16–17 January 1929. This involved two forces, Blue and Red, each with their own air assets. Four aircraft carriers took part, representing a large proportion of the Royal Navy's carrier strength at the time – these were *Argus*, *Courageous*, *Eagle* and *Furious*. The objective was for Blue to attempt to isolate and destroy a portion of the Red fleet, while Red had to protect two convoys.

A number of air attacks were carried out, by both sides, with Flycatchers generally providing escort to attacking forces as well as diversionary and flak-suppression attacks, but in one case, staging an attack by themselves on an enemy aircraft carrier. The first air attack was made at 0713 when torpedo bombers of 463 Flight, HMS *Courageous* air group, attacked Blue battle cruisers. Four minutes later, more torpedo bombers from the same Flight attacked HMS *Furious*. At 0758 Blue turned the tables with a concentrated torpedo attack of 12 aircraft from 461 and 462 Flights from *Furious*, on Red battle cruisers. Finally, at 0804, Flycatchers of 405 Flight carried out an attack on HMS *Courageous*.[14]

Later in the day, a further series of air attacks took place. At 0957, torpedo aircraft from three Flights, of *Courageous* and *Eagle*, attacked battleships of the Blue fleet, scoring multiple hits, while a second attack at 1314 was also successful. Meanwhile, at 1132, aircraft from *Furious* attacked battleships in the Red fleet and succeeded in 'reducing its speed' by 2 knots.[15]

Owen Cathcart-Jones described an incident during the exercise when 404 Flight caught HMS *Eagle*'s 402 Flight by surprise: "We had already gained considerable altitude and were hiding up in the direct line of the sun, thus making it extremely difficult for our climbing attackers to locate us. When everything was ready for the

12. Fish, T.W., Floats on the Flight Deck, Flight International 11 September 1969, p.428.
13. HMS Glorious, Flight, 16 May 1930, p.541.
14. Halpern, Paul G. (editor), The Mediterranean Fleet, 1919-1929, Ashgate Publishing, Ltd., 2011 p.550.
15. Halpern, Paul G. (editor), The Mediterranean Fleet, 1919-1929, Ashgate Publishing, Ltd., 2011 p.551.

The Royal Navy had a vast presence in the Mediterranean in the interwar period. Here the Mediterranean and Atlantic fleets assemble in Pollensa Bay, Mallorca, between 19 and 23 March 1929 for combined exercises. The aircraft carriers HMS Eagle *and HMS* Courageous *are in the furthermost row of ships at the right of the picture. (Author's collection)*

attack 'Skins' – our nickname for Lieutenant Commander Atkinson – gave us the signal by waving his hands. Then, each selecting his own opponent, we dived to attack. For the next few minutes, the sky was thick with small aircraft buzzing round each other like flies".

Policing Palestine

While the Flycatcher Flights would not have the opportunity to carry these attacks out for real, a demonstration was soon made as a deterrent during a period of violence in Mandatory Palestine.

Great Britain held a 'mandate' from the League of Nations to administer Palestine after its creation out of Ottoman Syria following the First World War. The increasing numbers of Jewish settlers had led to tensions between them and the indigenous Arab peoples, who perceived the immigrants as a threat. This came on top of anger arising from the perception that the British had reneged on promises of Arab independence in return for help defeating the Turks during the war. These tensions came to a head in 1929 over access to the Wailing Wall (also known as the Western or Buraq Wall) in Jerusalem, a site sacred to both Muslim and Jewish religions.

A Flycatcher landing aboard HMS Courageous *in the Mediterranean around 1928-29, taken by Flying Officer Marescaux. When* Courageous *was commissioned as an aircraft carrier, she could carry 48 aircraft, a large complement by Royal Navy standards. This was aided by the small size of the Flycatcher saving hangar space, despite its lack of folding wings. The running deck crew are preparing to catch the aircraft and bring it to a stop before wheeling it to the lift, necessary as the aircraft had neither wheel brakes nor a steerable tailskid. (Author's collection)*

Violence erupted after demonstrations at the wall and quickly spread across Jerusalem and beyond. In Hebron (al-Khalīl) around 65 Jews were killed when the Jewish Quarter was attacked by a mob. At the time, the British authorities had few troops in Palestine and only a handful of armoured cars and aircraft. Reinforcements were summoned from the army and RAF across the Middle East and Mediterranean. HMS *Courageous* was ordered to transport a Battalion and artillery of the South Staffordshire regiment, and lend support with her air group and naval landing parties. *Courageous* arrived at Haifa on the morning of 28 August.

Immediately on arriving, *Courageous* flew off six Flycatchers of 404 Flight and a Fairey IIIF to aid the RAF on shore. From Ramleh, 402 Flight started flying patrols over the desert searching for the perpetrators of the violence in Hebron, and to try to keep separate groups of Jewish settlers and Arabs. "At the first sign of violence," wrote Owen Catchcart-Jones, "our instructions were to try to separate the conflicting parties and then take offensive action."[16]

This patrol was uneventful, but immediately afterwards, the Flight was sent to Jerusalem to make a 'show of force' over the city. "We were soon over this marvellous city," Catchart-Jones wrote, "and went through a practice run of one of our converging bombing attacks on the Mosque in the centre of the city, under the shadow of the Mount of Olives.[17] The 'Blue Note' of the Flycatchers greatly impressed the people in the crowded streets below."[18]

The following morning, reports of violence against a Jewish settlement near Jaffa were received. The perpetrators were believed to have ridden into the desert with a camel train, so 404 Flight was dispatched to disrupt

16. Cathcart-Jones, Owen, Aviation Memoirs, Hutchinson & Co. 1934. p.180.
17. Presumably, from the description, the Dome of the Rock.
18. Cathcart-Jones, Owen, Aviation Memoirs, Hutchinson & Co. 1934. p.180.

Aircraft from HMS Courageous, *having landed at the RAF airfield at Gaza on 1 April 1929. Most of the aircraft are Fairey IIIF spotter/reconnaissance types, but to the extreme right, two Flycatchers of 404 Flight can be seen. The Flycatchers were employed making 'shows of force', disrupting camel trains and scouting for fleeing rioters. (Author's collection)*

their escape. "The only transport across the desert," Cathcart-Jones explained, "is by camel train, its beasts being frequently changed from the loose herd which accompany the tribe. With its camels removed, transport comes to a standstill, and the offending tribe is easily captured.

"Against this tribe we were sent out on an offensive patrol, with instructions to dive at the herd of camel, scare them into bolting across the desert, and thus leave the Arabs without transport. Land forces operating in armoured cars would then round them up and bring them to justice.

"We thought this kind of flying too good to be true and set off on our errand full of glee. For an area of some 200 square miles there wasn't a camel in the whole of Palestine which hadn't been zoomed and dived at in our efforts to disperse them. If we came across a large herd of camels grazing anywhere on the dry grass and shrubs of the desert, all three of us would dive at them and round them up. Then, by firing Verey signal cartridges on to the ground, we set fire to the dry grass, thus driving the camels into the desert, where they scattered in all directions."[19]

It is unclear how successful 404 Flight's efforts were in helping with the apprehension of the perpetrators of violence in Hebron. The episode does at least demonstrate the controllability of the Flycatcher, in that it was possible to co-ordinate aircraft in this way.

On the end of August, the carrier was ordered to fly off all aircraft except two 'S/R' (spotting and reconnaissance) machines to Gaza, and to prepare to land Flight stores and personnel for transport to support them.

19. Cathcart-Jones, Owen, Aviation Memoirs, Hutchinson & Co. 1934, p.180.

Initially the aircraft prepared to make a formation demonstration flight in force over Palestine, but information from the High Commissioner suggested the aircraft were urgently needed for reconnaissance and operations over Southern Palestine. On 30 and 31 August, aircraft from *Courageous* carried out reconnaissance and patrols to the South of Latitude 31° 30' N and along the Jordan Valley.[20]

Aircraft from *Courageous* subsequently undertook patrols, conducted 'shows of force' and provided air support to ground operations aimed at preventing violence and hunting down perpetrators of violence. It was believed that some of those responsible for the attacks in Hebron were hiding in the village of El Weleje near Jerusalem. Two platoons of the South Wales Borderers with Palestine Police were detailed to surround the village and capture the ringleaders, supported by Fleet Air Arm Flights from Gaza.

To help the aircraft identify the correct village, the Air Liaison Intelligence Officer travelled there shortly before dawn to place canvas strips in a prominent place on the rocky ground, while a cordon of troops took positions on the outskirts.

In a similar manner to the combined operation in Bias Bay two years previously, the Flycatchers from *Courageous* were required to circle overhead and fire on anyone attempting to flee.

A number of similar raids were carried out with the presence of the Flycatchers overhead, though they never had to fire on anyone. Even so, over 100 Arabs are believed to have been killed during the British crackdown following the riots and attacks.

By the middle of September, the threat of violence appeared to be waning, while the senior naval officers present began to worry that the efficiency of the ships would be compromised if such large proportions of their companies remained ashore much longer.[21] *Courageous* re-embarked all Flights and proceeded on an independent cruise. This included a 'flag-flying' visit to Turkey, where the ship's Flycatchers and IIIFs flew over Istambul in a formation shaped like a crescent and star on 18 October as a salute to the Turkish people and government.

20. Halpern, Paul G. (editor), The Mediterranean Fleet, 1919-1929, Ashgate Publishing, Ltd., 2011 p.574.
21. Halpern, Paul G. (editor), The Mediterranean Fleet, 1919-1929, Ashgate Publishing, Ltd., 2011 p.574.

Five Flycatchers of 407 Flight attached to HMS Courageous *in 1927. Closest to the camera is N9948 coded '4', then N9926 (no code), N9924 '1', N9945 '2' and N9943 '6'. The fuselage bands are light blue, worn when Courageous was stationed in the Mediterranean Fleet until it returned home in 1930, after which 407 Flight transferred to HMS* Furious *and its codes change to three digit numbers beginning with 5. (ARCHIVE Images, www.archive-images.co.uk)*

Flycatcher N9962 '2' of 405 Flight takes off from the main flying deck of HMS Furious, *with another aircraft of the Flight waiting behind.* Furious *was the first fleet carrier in the Royal Navy, having been converted from a lightly-armoured battle cruiser known as a 'large light cruiser'. (Fleet Air Arm Museum)*

To have switched from potential offensive missions during an outbreak of violence to an exuberant display of peacetime flying in little over a month seems to encapsulate the Flycatcher's career with the Fleet Air Arm.

While the Flycatcher flights never had the chance to attempt in anger the 'converging bombing' (and strafing) attacks they had developed, there were plenty of opportunities to use them to impress the public. These demonstration attacks became a favourite feature of RAF Air Pageants at Hendon in the 1920s and 1930s. The display of June 1931 was described by 'Flight':

"An encampment of four white tents had been observed and it had evidently aroused the wrath of HMS *Courageous*, which sent No. 407 (Fleet Fighter) Flight to obliterate it. The five 'Flycatcher' Fighters appeared suddenly in V formation and dived wrathfully upon the innocent-looking bell tents. After giving them a preliminary burst of combined fire, the flight formed a circle up above, from which one 'Flycatcher' was always diving onto the camp. As it zoomed up, exposing its tail to the ground gunners, another machine from a different part of the circle would come down with its guns snapping out blanks. One could never tell from which the next attack would come, and the ground gunners must have been equally at sea. Such an attack is very difficult to counter, but it must take infinite practice and understanding between the pilots to work it up to such a stage of perfection... After a while the flight took to hand bombs in place of machine guns, and soon two of the tents were blazing so merrily that the fire brigade had to work hard to beat out the fire in the grass."

The 'converging bombing' attack had been superseded by the time the Fleet Air Arm went to war in 1939, and it is doubtful that it would have been effective against targets defended by anti-aircraft artillery. However, against a relatively uncoordinated force equipped only with small arms, it could well have been devastating.

The Flycatcher's largely unsung 'colonial policing' work continued. It may not have been combat, strictly speaking, but it could still be dangerous. On 21 December 1931, Lieutenant P.D. Heineman of 406 Flight died when he crashed floatplane-configured Flycatcher N9670 during a show of force "to compel [the] Sultan of Muscat to pay taxes." The aircraft made a series of low-level runs near the cruiser HMS *Emerald*, where the Sultan had been summoned, and was seen to make a "downward plunge" during one of these runs and struck the sea. Heineman died in the cockpit.[22]

22. Moore, J.H., caption to photographs in the archive of the Fleet Air Arm Museum.

Flycatchers of HMS Furious' *'slip flight' running up their engines before taking off. The aircraft have their 'flaperons' lowered for maximum lift, and a crewmember at each wingtip to guide them as they taxi forward. This was helpful in the case of the Flycatcher, which had no wheel brakes or steerable tailskid to aid control at low speeds. The foremost aircraft, coded '17', has a camera gun attached to its lower starboard mainplane, as well as having a Vickers gun fitted to the fuselage side. (Fleet Air Arm Museum)*

Flycatcher N9866 takes off from the lower flying deck of HMS Furious. *The three 'large light cruisers' were all converted with a short flight deck at the bow that connected directly with the upper hangar. Flycatchers, known as the 'slip flight' could be flown off directly from the hangar, taking advantage of the short take-off roll required by the Flycatcher – though this image shows just how quickly the aircraft taking off could run out of deck. (Fleet Air Arm Museum)*

Flycatchers of 405 Flight, HMS Furious *air group, ashore in 1929. All aircraft are fitted with spinners and the short cowling ring covering the Jaguar engine's reduction gear. The nearest aircraft, N9933, which wore the code '10' while with 405 Flight, was later stationed at RAF Hal Far, and was written off when it ditched off Zurrieq with Lieutenant F.E. Judd at the controls. Judd escaped with minor injuries. (Fleet Air Arm Museum)*

Flycatcher N9935 '16' of 405 Flight, being recovered off Torbay onto HMS Furious*, on 29 June 1927. The aircraft had crashed off the ship into the sea. It does not appear to have sustained significant damage, though apparently it was written off as a result of the accident. (Author's collection)*

A Flycatcher landing aboard HMS Glorious *or* Courageous. *The recovery crew can be seen poised along the edge of the flight deck, ready to run in and stop the fighter, prevent it from slewing to one side, and wheel it to the lift. The image shows how much space the small Flycatcher had when landing aboard a large fleet carrier. (Steve Moorey collection)*

A moment that indicates the hazards of landing aboard a carrier in a fairly lightly-loaded aircraft. Flight Lieutenant W Sanderson, commander of 407 Flight (note the streamers on the interplane struts), picks up a gust while landing on HMS Courageous *during a period of embarkation in September–November 1930. The Flycatcher flew off the deck and crashed in the sea. Fortunately, Sanderson was picked up unharmed by an accompanying destroyer. (Author's collection)*

A well-known photograph of Flycatcher N9928, by the photographer Charles E. Brown in 1930, sporting unusual markings on the rear decking and wheels. The aircraft was part of the Miscellaneous Flight at RAF Hal Far, Malta until June that year, later transferring to 401 Flight, HMS Courageous. *(Author's collection)*

Another well-known image of J9928, this time over the aircraft carrier HMS Eagle. *This vessel was a battleship converted to a carrier during construction and in the 1920s and early 1930s served largely in the Mediterranean. The only Flycatcher Flight formally attached to* Eagle's *air group was 402 Flight, which N9928 does not appear to have been assigned to, despite the caption often appearing with this image 'HMS* Eagle *with aircraft up'. (Author's collection)*

Flycatcher S1280 taking off from the lower flight deck on HMS Glorious, *on what is evidently a rough day judging from the amount of water on the deck. This aircraft flew from* Glorious *with both 408 Flight, when it wore the code '9', from 1929–31, and 406 Flight thereafter. The fuselage band is actually yellow, despite its dark appearance, the result of orthochromatic film rendering some colours as black. (Author's collection)*

'Hermes Children ready To Play Malta 22 November 1930' reads the caption on the album this photograph was originally part of. It shows Flycatchers of 403 Flight lining up on the deck of the carrier, demonstrating the diagonal white fuselage bands to good effect. The Flight numbered its aircraft 1-9 until 1932, when it adopted three-digit codes beginning with 5. The first aircraft here is '4', followed by '6' and '5'. (Author's collection)

Flycatcher '7' of 406 Flight, HMS Glorious, *rigged as a floatplane. Note the flight-leader's streamers on the upper wing trailing edges. The upper wing stripes appear to have been marred by roughly doped patches. (Author's collection)*

HMS Glorious *was the third of the 'large light cruisers' to begin conversion into an aircraft carrier, and was largely similar to* Courageous, *with an island to starboard unlike the flush-deck* Furious. *She re-commissioned in that role in 1930, and after a short spell with the Home Fleet, mainly served in the Mediterranean. She operated Flycatchers of 405 and 406 Flights from 1930 until Flycatchers were phased out in 1934. (Author's collection)*

An odd image of Flycatcher's landing aboard HMS Glorious *in the Mediterannean in 1932, seemingly with a small sailing boat sitting on the deck just where the first aircraft is about to touch down! The impression has been caused by a double exposure, with the boat and island of Malta appearing on the same image as Flycatchers landing. (Author's collection)*

Aircraft of the Station Flight from RAF Hal Far, Malta, in formation in May 1932, showing a cross-section of the types then operating with the Fleet Air Arm and RAF. From top to bottom, a Flycatcher, Blackburn Ripon, de Havilland DH60 Moth, Fairey IIIF, Avro 504N, Ripon, Hawker Osprey (a type then in the process of replacing the Flycatcher as the Fleet Air Arm's main single-seat fighter). (Author's collection)

A large formation of 13 Flycatchers above RAF Hal Far and the distinctive Maltese landscape in 1932. The formation is likely to be to mark an event such as Empire Day, as it must include aircraft of more than one Flight. Aircraft from 405 Flight, HMS Glorious, *are almost certainly involved as the photographer, Flying Officer Marescaux, was based aboard the ship at the time, flying spotter-reconnaissance aircraft. (Author's collection)*

Another Flycatcher crash at RAF Hal Far, this time of aircraft '20' (possibly N9862, in which case it had already survived one forced landing) of 405 Flight in 1930–31. The engine has ended up some distance from the fuselage. The fuselage stripe appears dark, but this is an artefact of the type of film used – it is actually yellow. (Author's collection)

Not all Flycatcher mishaps took place on shore. This photograph shows a ditched 405 Flight Flycatcher being towed into Kalafrana, Malta, by an RAF pinnace. Flycatchers carried flotation bags in their rear fuselages and could often be recovered after ditching. The aircraft does not seem to be badly damaged. (Author's collection)

A Flycatcher ashore. This aircraft wears the markings of 402 Flight, part of HMS Courageous' *air group. The steeply aft-sloping fuselage band is pale blue, and the tail fin black. The crest on the fin appears to be the crossed winged swords and trident later used by 800 Squadron, into which 402 Flight and 404 Flight were merged in 1933. (Author's collection)*

Another Flycatcher of 402 Flight wearing similar markings to the previous photograph. This machine is N9662, coded '507'. According to a caption in Aeroplane Monthly of December 1976, the pilot is "our friend 'Rupert' in trouble again, this time being retrieved after nearly going 'over the end'". Note the gun camera fitted to the lower starboard mainplane. N9662 was a long-lived Flycatcher – one of the earliest aircraft from the first large production batch, it was still on charge in 1933 (see earlier photograph of the same aircraft). (Author's collection)

Mishaps in Flycatchers were not uncommon but the aircraft was so strongly built and relatively light that it could often be repaired and return to service. Here, N9676 '10' of 407 Flight, HMS Courageous *air group, can be seen after nosing over at Hal Far in Malta in 1928 or 1929. This was actually N9676's third incident, following a forced landing in a field near Leuchars in February 1924 and a fractured tailskid leading to a broken longeron aboard HMS* Hermes *in July that year. The aircraft was repaired after its crash in Malta and later flew with 404 and 402 Flights. (Steve Moorey collection)*

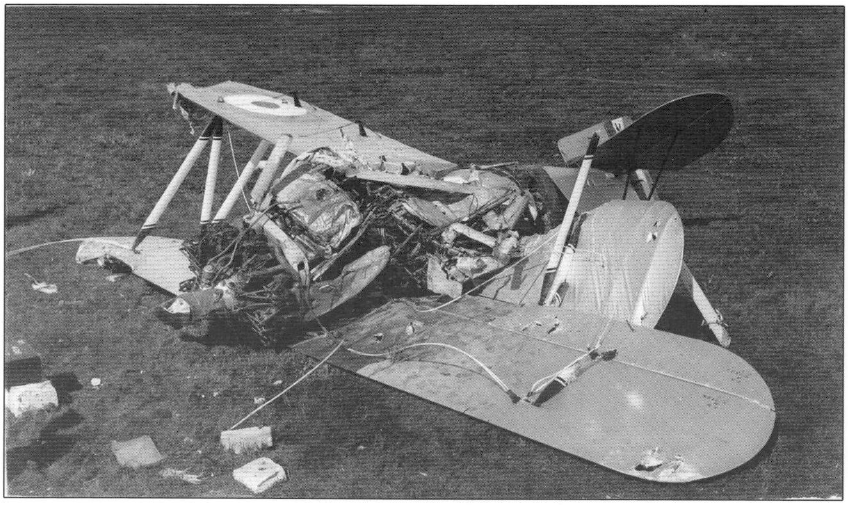

The wreckage of comprehensively destroyed Flycatcher N9904 of 406 Flight, which crashed at Hal Far on 18 February 1932 when pilot Flying Officer Tillard stalled and crashed into a boundary wall. (Steve Moorey collection)

Two more images of the wreckage of N9904 at Hal Far. The Flycatcher's strong construction and modest performance saved a number of pilots in crashes, and this was the case here – despite the thoroughly destroyed airframe, Tillard escaped with minor injuries. (Author's collection)

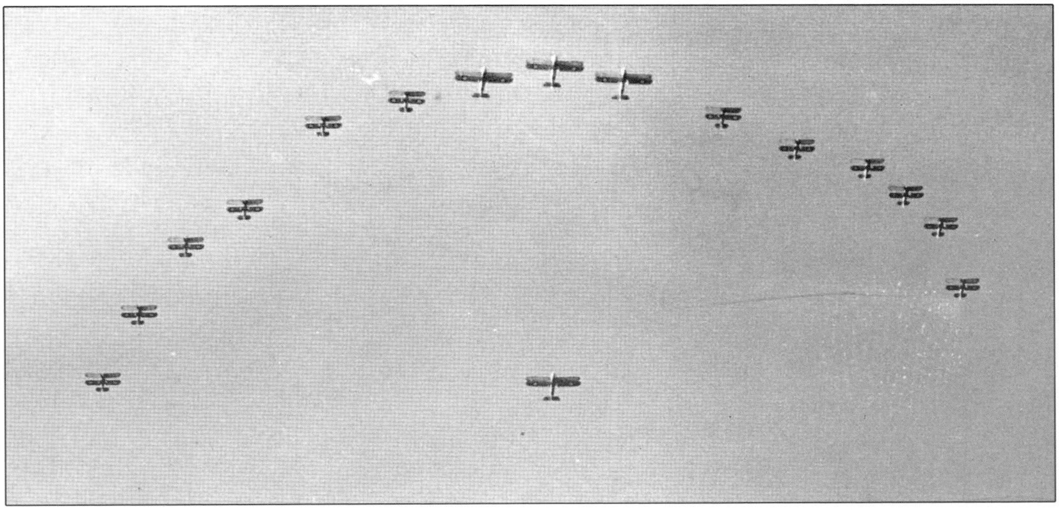

In September 1931, HMS Courageous *made a courtesy visit to Turkey, and her aircraft – Fairey IIIF spotter-reconnaissance aircraft and Flycatcher fighters – flew over Istanbul in a 'crescent and star' formation as a salute to the city. (Steve Moorey collection)*

A sequence of photographs showing HMS Berwick's *Flycatcher floatplane being launched from its catapult, then recovered. Flycatchers of 403 Flight provided aircraft to the 5th Cruiser Squadron, which was made up of HMS* Berwick, *HMS* Cornwall, *HMS* Cumberland, *HMS* Kent *and HMS* Suffolk, *from 1930. The aircraft used were from the small batch of catapult-stressed Flycatchers. (Author's collection)*

Flycatchers took part in a number of fleet exercises; indeed, this was the closest the type got to conventional air combat. This cartoon indicates Fleet Air Arm personnel's view of these exercises and the competition between carriers – in this case the near-sisters HMS Furious *and HMS* Courageous. *The cartoon evokes the description of a dogfight from one such exercises – "each selecting his own opponent, we dived to attack. For the next few minutes, the sky was thick with small aircraft buzzing round each other like flies." (Steve Moorey collection)*

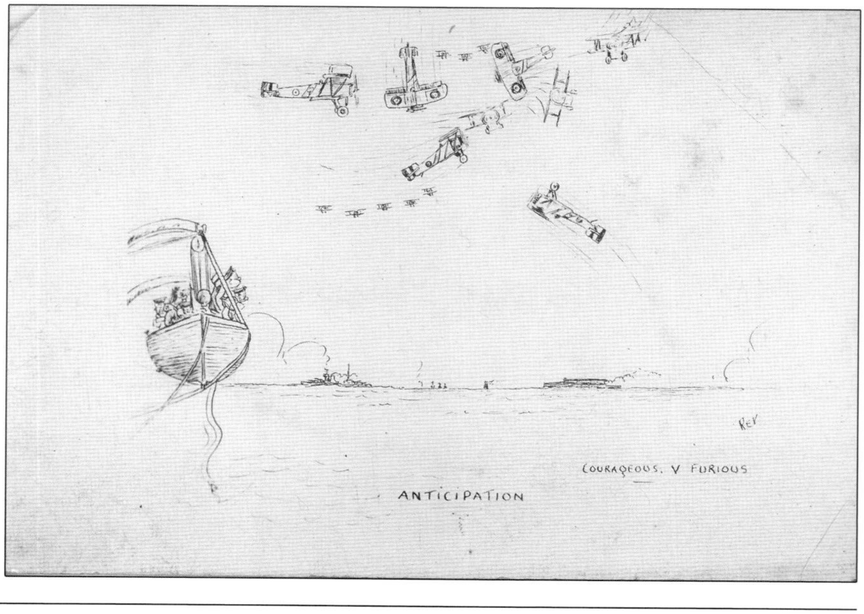

While Flycatchers never formally went into action, they made a great many public demonstrations of the tactics and methods they would have used if called upon to do so, at home and abroad. Here a Flycatcher '3' of 402 Flight, HMS Eagle, *demonstrates the phenomenal accuracy of its dive-bombing ability, by destroying a model house with a direct hit at the Hal Far Air Pageant on 25 May 1929. (Fleet Air Arm Museum)*

After serving as a conventional Fleet Fighter Flight, 406 Flight was temporarily disbanded in 1932, then re-formed the following year to provide floatplanes for the 4th Cruiser Squadron made up of HMS Enterprise *and HMS* Emerald *(now fitted with catapults in place of revolving platforms). Floatplane S1291 is seen here in May 1933, being craned from the water after a flight. Even this late in the Flycatcher's career, the older square wooden floats are still in use. A floatplane from the Flight was lost, and its pilot Lieutenant Heineman, killed. (Author's collection)*

Advancing the state of the art

The Flycatcher itself may have been out-of-date by the time it left front-line service in 1932, but it played a crucial role in helping the Fleet Air Arm stay at the cutting edge between the wars. Over its decade-long career, the little fighter helped the RN improve its deck-landing practices, launching techniques and technology, fighting tactics and organisation.

The Flycatcher was among the first aircraft to benefit from what later became known as a 'technical publication'. Fairey realised that the increasing complexity of aircraft meant that clear communication between manufacturer and customer was essential, and that units in the field needed precise information about every aspect of the aircraft's construction for day-to-day operations. The company produced a loose-leaf book with detailed descriptions of each component and perspective drawings of each structure and sub-assembly. Each component was listed and numbered, with numbers corresponding to the manufacturer's stores. These were issued to every unit and establishment operating Flycatchers. This format was soon common practice with the Air Ministry, which produced a guide with the aid of manufacturers for every aircraft and engine accepted into service. It would be another 20 years before similarly formal sets of notes for the aid of pilots was available.

During the late 1920s and early 1930s, the 'flying-off platforms' that had been fitted to cruisers and battleships were superseded by catapults, which could accelerate aircraft to flying speed irrespective of the wind over the deck. The heavy cruiser HMS Suffolk *was fitted with a 'SIIL' (Slider Mk.II) type catapult in 1931, and the first aircraft carried was a Flycatcher. Flycatcher S1413, seen here on* Suffolk's *catapult, was part of a batch of Flycatchers delivered specifically with catapult operations in mind. (Author's collection)*

Platforms and catapults

The Flycatcher was born into an area of aviation that was developing rapidly. The continuous-deck aircraft carrier had existed for less than five years when it first flew, and the science of flying aircraft from standard warships was only marginally more advanced. Over its career, a number of Flycatchers were assigned to trials and experiments, and the experiences of service units added further to the advance of naval aviation.

Towards the end of the First World War, the RN had developed the means to fly landplanes off warships using revolving platforms as mini flying-off decks that could be pointed into wind partly independent of the ship's direction. This was still orthodoxy when the Flycatcher entered service, although the increasing weight and size of military aircraft was making the practice less and less practical. Fairey prioritised structural strength with the Flycatcher at the expense of its ability to fly from such platforms – an increase in available engine power made a considerable improvement.

Trials were carried out from a mock-up platform on the deck of HMS *Argus*, following experimentation at the National Physical Laboratory's wind-tunnel, and later 'live' tests were carried out from HMS *Caledon*. These proved that the use of platforms was still valid despite the increasing size and weight of naval fighters.

Interestingly, during the Flycatcher's trials aboard HMS *Argus* in 1924 it was found that launching the aircraft tail-down was preferable to the more usual method of propping the aircraft level with a trestle. It would be another twenty years before the RN would rediscover the benefits of 'tail-down' launching from aircraft carrier accelerators after years persisting with complex cradles to hold the aircraft in flying attitude. Despite earlier misgivings, Flycatchers served successfully from warship platforms until they were withdrawn from service in the early 1930s.

Flycatcher S1413 being launched from HMS Suffolk's *catapult while on the China station in 1932, fitted with the more modern duralumin floats first tested on a Flycatcher in 1926. (Author's collection)*

An unidentified Flycatcher of 403 Flight with the cruiser HMS Cumberland, *of the 5th Cruiser Squadron. In January 1933, 403 Flight was enlarged to provide aircraft and crews for the Squadron's cruisers.* Cumberland *retained her Flycatcher until April 1935. This aircraft has the older style wooden floats, and carries the badge of HMS* Cumberland *on its fin. The upper centre-section is painted in red and white checks. (Fleet Air Arm Museum)*

By the mid-1920s, however, Fairey's insistence on making the Flycatcher as strong as possible was borne out when the RN started to switch to catapults in place of the revolving platforms. Catapults powered by compressed air, and subsequently by cordite charges, were developed at the Royal Aircraft Establishment at Farnborough to hurl aircraft bodily into the air. The first practical Carey-type catapult was fitted to HMS *Vindictive* where it was extensively tested. Flycatcher floatplane N9913 was trialled from the cruiser in 1925, which proved the aircraft's suitability and detachments of Flycatchers later served aboard catapult-equipped ships from 1926. It says much for the Flycatcher's qualities that it was the only type that was operated routinely from both turret platforms and catapults, and this undoubtedly helped the RN transition between the two systems.

On 26 November 1929, a Flycatcher became the first Fleet Air Arm fighter to perform a night landing aboard an aircraft carrier. This had been attempted with Blackburn Dart torpedo bombers and Fairey IIIF reconnaissance aircraft before, but the first such landing by a fighter was apparently carried out by Flying Officer Keary and Owen Cathcart-Jones of 404 Flight, while *Courageous* was steaming off Malta.[1]

Aside from the disorientating effects of the flight deck seeming to float 'disembodied' in the blackness of sea and sky, the landings were made without difficulty and repeated three times before the Flycatchers returned to Hal Far. It is another testament to the docile handling and deck-landing abilities of the Flycatcher that the first night landing of a single seat fighter aboard a Royal Navy aircraft carrier at sea were made without any problems at all.

1. Cathcart-Jones, Owen, Aviation Memoirs, Hutchinson & Co. 1934, p.186.

As naval aircraft became ever larger and heavier, it also became necessary to find ways to accelerate take-off in calm conditions. Flycatchers (including N9947) were used to test the RAE's compressed-air powered accelerator[2] between 1928 and 1933, their robust construction again proving ideal. This formed the basis of the systems which would be used on British aircraft carriers until the jet age. The Flycatchers of the final production batch, S1409 to S1418, were distinguished as 'catapult type' in the order of March 1930.[3]

Metal floats and airscrews

In July 1927, a Flycatcher and a Fairey IIIF, flown by Flight Lieutenants Mackintosh and Barlow, took part in some very unusual exercises aboard HMS *Furious*. These trials involved both landing and taking off on the carrier's flight deck with floats fitted. These were the duralumin floats with a 'V'-section planing bottom that had been introduced as an improvement on the previously standard flat-bottomed wooden pontoon-type items. The floats had been strengthened at the base but were not fitted with wheels of any kind – the trials appear to have had the objective of ascertaining whether 'pure' floatplanes could operate from the deck of an aircraft carrier.

The Flycatcher, N9619, being the smaller and lighter, was the first of the two aircraft to attempt a landing and take-off, with three of each being successfully carried out. The deck had been thoroughly greased and the Flycatcher was able to take off with the aid of the flight deck party rocking and shoving to break the friction.

2. 'Accelerators' differed from catapults in the Royal Navy's view as they assisted the take-off of an aircraft along a runway or flight deck, as opposed to catapults, which aircraft were usually mounted on by crane, to be launched into flight.
3. Sturtivant, R. and Cronin, D., Fleet Air Arm Aircraft, Units and Ships 1920 to 1939, Air Britain 1998, p. 176.

In 1932, Flycatcher N9673 was tested with a metal Fairey-Reed airscrew and duralumin floats with water rudders, at the Marine Aeroplane Experimental Establishment at Felixstowe, where it is seen here. The tests were designed to determine the effects of the airscrew and floats on manoeuvrability in the air and on the water. (Author's collection)

Landings were more spectacular – T.W. Fish of 462 Flight watched the proceedings: "I can recollect that as I watched from the safety nets alongside the deck I could see a shower of sparks from the contact of the reinforced floats with the steel deck as the aircraft slid along upon landing", he later wrote.[4]

The landings were successful with the shortest taking 170 ft, while the longest was 214 ft. The take-offs required up to 198 ft of deck in a 26 kt headwind. This compares with as low as 20 ft for take-off and 50 ft for landing with wheel undercarriage depending on conditions. The floats were found to have suffered slight crushing at the bulkhead of the after step, but no serious damage. It is not clear what use the Navy put the findings of these trials to, although the practice of landing a floatplane on the deck of an aircraft carrier did find some favour. During the early part of the Second World War, for example, it was not unknown for Swordfish floatplanes to land directly on aircraft carriers when delivering an urgent message or if the carrier could not spare the time to recover the floatplane in the conventional way.

In 1932, Flycatcher N9673 was tested with a metal Fairey-Reed airscrew and floats similar to those used in the *Furious* tests, with water rudders, at the Marine Aeroplane Experimental Establishment at Felixstowe.[5] The tests were designed to determine the effects of the airscrew and floats on manoeuvrability in the air and on the water. The aircraft's general handling was tested, and climbs at various speeds made. The overall weight was 3,615 lb.

Spinning tests were carried out first, in July and August, by Flight Lieutenant Pickering and Flying Officer Snaith. The floats and airscrew had not unduly affected spinning characteristics, apart from when the tail incidence was set fully back ('down'). Recovery could be effected within half a turn of taking the usual anti-spin measures, although in some circumstances spins to the left, in the direction of propeller rotation, were found to be 'jerky'.[6]

Flying characteristics were found to be similar to Flycatchers fitted with wooden, flat-bottomed floats. The floats slightly improved the aircraft's longitudinal stability in a dive. Manoeuvrability on the water was found to be very good, aided by the water rudders which were operated by their own controls, unconnected to the main rudder. The water rudders were steered using a lever fitted to the starboard side of the cockpit. This made it easy for the aircraft to approach a slipway even in adverse wind and sea conditions. The only downside was the amount of water thrown up by the floats onto the propeller during taxiing, and the MAEE recommended the fitting of wider chine strips to deflect some of the spray.

During take-offs, the MAEE found it was better for the oleo to be set to provide a slow rebound, and in that condition, take-offs and landings were found to be easy. The metal airscrew gave an acceptable performance.

Although it was not part of the tests, the MAEE remarked that the Flycatcher flew in a somewhat tail-down manner, and the adjustable tailplane did not fully alleviate this even when fully 'up', while the extremity of the 'down' setting was never required. They recommended adjusting the range of the device, although it is not known whether this was ever carried out given that replacement of the aircraft was already well underway.

4. Fish, T.W., Floats on the Flight Deck, Flight International 11 September 1969, p.428.
5. Short performance tests on Flycatcher N9673, under AVIA 19/552, National Archives.
6. Spinning tests on Flycatcher seaplane, under AVIA 19/552, National Archives.

The End

The Air Staff was optimistic that significantly better aircraft would be available within a few years of the Flycatcher's entry into service, and that the Flycatcher's ascendency would be brief. The reality would prove somewhat different. A new requirement was issued by the Air Ministry in 1926. Specification 21/26 demanded 'greatly improved performance' and insisted that the new aircraft be powered by the new Bristol Mercury supercharged nine-cylinder radial engine. An interchangeable float and wheel undercarriage was once again specified. There were thirteen entries from ten manufacturers, including Fairey.[1] The Fairey submission was called the Flycatcher II – in fact a completely new biplane with some family resemblance to the original Flycatcher.

Fairey had expended considerable effort in the early 1920s to develop the state of the art in military aircraft. This stemmed partly from the ungainly Fawn bomber, which appalled Sir Richard Fairey who felt that contemporary Air Ministry specifications were, for various reasons, leading to poor aeroplanes. At the same time, the American entries for the Schneider Trophy showed the performance possible by matching aerodynamically clean airframes with powerful liquid-cooled engines of low frontal area. The Fox bomber was followed by the conceptually similar Firefly single-seat fighter which, unlike the Fox, was not ordered by the RAF.

1. Meekcoms, K.J. and Morgan, E.B., The British Aircraft Specification Files 1920-49, Air Britain 1994, p.107.

The Admiralty began to look for a replacement for the Flycatcher almost as soon as it had come into service, in 1926. Fairey's answer was the Flycatcher II, effectively a new aeroplane developed from the experience gained with the original Flycatcher – notably the use of steel tubing in the structure and the effective oleo-pneumatic undercarriage. The prototype N216 is seen here with an interim engine installation of an Armstrong Siddeley Jaguar instead of the preferred Bristol Mercury, which was not available when the aircraft first flew. (Author's collection)

The sole Flycatcher II prototype could be easily converted into a floatplane, as could the original aircraft. Here N216 is seen in flight with duralumin floats fitted. The family resemblance to the original Flycatcher is apparent, despite the much cleaner aerodynamics. The aircraft was wrecked in a crash in 1929, by which time the Air Ministry had indicated that it had no further interest in the aircraft. (Author's collection)

The Flycatcher II was externally similar to the Firefly. Unlike the earlier slab-sided Flycatcher, the new aircraft had a clean, rounded fuselage, into which the two Vickers guns were now completely faired. The wing cellule was single-bay, with a lower wing somewhat smaller than the upper, and little stagger. The upper centre-section was bowed upward for greater forward visibility. The chief difference between the Firefly and the Flycatcher II was that the latter had a fully all-metal structure while the former was still largely of wood-framed construction, and the naval aircraft was powered by an air-cooled radial engine. The undercarriage was a streamlined V arrangement that retained the long-stroke capability necessary on a naval aircraft.

The Flycatcher II first flew with a Jaguar powerplant, but this was later changed for the preferred engine, the new supercharged Bristol Mercury. The nine-cylinder Mercury allowed a very clean installation, with a pointed nose completely fairing the reduction gear and crankcase and leaving only the cylinders exposed.

Unfortunately, the Mercury was too early in its development to meet the demands made of it, and most of the prototypes were fitted with different powerplants during their development. It seems the Air Ministry was unimpressed with the designs offered, especially with the specified radial engines failing to allow the naval fighters to compete with inline-engined land-fighters. Nevertheless, the top speed of the Mercury-engined Flycatcher II is given as 153 mph, 20 mph faster than the original Flycatcher and similar to the contemporary American Curtiss F6C naval fighter (although 12 mph slower than the competing Gloster Gnatsnapper with the same powerplant). The Flycatcher II could reach speeds of 144 mph with the alternative floatplane undercarriage. At some stage during the trials, N216 was fitted with a broader-chord fin, suggesting a lack of directional stability in the original configuration.

A further specification (32/26) was issued later in the year for the development of the Flycatcher II, though unfortunately it is unclear what the Air Ministry required. The specification was archived in January 1929, indicating that there was no further interest in the Flycatcher II.[2] The sole prototype, N216, crashed and was written off in May that year and no further development was carried out, as Fairey was now committed to its Firefly biplane family both for land and naval fighter projects.

However, during this time, the experience of the Flycatcher II seems at least to have persuaded Fairey that its structure was worth pursuing in fighters of all kinds, and the Firefly was subsequently redesigned into the all-metal Firefly IIM (the M standing for metal), then the Mk.III.

A great deal of effort was expended trying to bring the 1926 designs up to the standard required by the FAA, including relaxing the requirement for a Mercury engine. (The Hawker design, for example, was tried with three engines, and the Gloster design with four, including both liquid-cooled and air-cooled powerplants). It would take another four years of development before a suitable design, the Hawker Norn (later developed into the Nimrod) was decided on, and a further four years before Flycatchers were finally replaced. Throughout this time the Flycatcher did everything that was asked of it, remained universally popular with crews, and proved an extremely difficult act to follow in a number of respects.

Nevertheless, by the early 1930s it was clear that the Flycatcher was overdue for replacement. RAF fighters were starting to reach speeds of 200 mph, nearly 70 mph faster than the Flycatcher and naval aircraft of other nations were starting to eclipse the Flycatcher by a significant margin. It had taken until 1930, seven years after the Flycatcher had entered service, for the FAA to name its successor, the Hawker Nimrod, and until 1932 for the Fleet Fighter Flights to begin to re-equip with that aircraft.

In addition to the Nimrod, the FAA introduced a two-seat type, the Osprey, from the same stable. The replacement of 404 Flight's Flycatchers with Ospreys in April 1932 marked the introduction of so-called Fighter-Reconnaissance Flights in the Fleet Air Arm. It is arguable that the move to two-seat fighter-reconnaissance types hampered the FAA for over a decade with design dead-ends like the Skua and Fulmar. It was only with the re-introduction of 'pure' purpose-designed naval single-seaters like the Grumman Martlet and Chance-Vought Corsair, the true heirs to the Flycatcher, that the service got its edge back. Against this background it is little surprise that the quirky, agile Flycatcher remains well-loved.

The Flycatcher's characteristics ideally suited it to develop the Fleet Air Arm's systems and technology over the ten years of its service. Its combination of strength, docile handling and adaptability helped the RN develop naval aviation from First World War thinking with longitudinal wires and turret platforms into the 1930s with catapults and accelerators.

The Flycatcher was, taken as a whole, a huge leap forward from the First World War types it replaced. It provided a reasonable increase in performance, while incorporating a multitude of small innovations which served to increase the aircraft's practicality, usefulness and effectiveness, and which made the lives of pilots and maintainers easier. Without these incremental improvements adding to the general perfection of the Flycatcher for its designed purpose, it may well not have lasted so long in frontline service.

2. Meekcoms, K.J. and Morgan, E.B., The British Aircraft Specification Files 1920-49, Air Britain 1994, p.112.

The Flycatcher was eventually replaced by the Hawker Nimrod, based on Hawker's earlier Hoopoe and Norn designs. This aircraft, K3661, flew with 802 Squadron in HMS Glorious' *air group, formed from 408 and 409 Flights, the former of which operated Flycatchers, also from* Glorious. *(Author)*

The only 'survivor'

For such an important aircraft within the Fleet Air Arm's history, it is perhaps surprising that there are no original Fairey Flycatchers in existence. There is, however, the closest possible substitute in the form of a replica built by the son of the Fairey firm's founder using original plans, and benefiting from the advice of Wilfred Broadbent, Fairey's works manager in the 1920s.[1]

John Fairey had been considering building or commissioning a replica Flycatcher after he sold Spitfire G-AIDN, which was becoming too expensive for him to operate.[2] A conversation with Viv Bellamy, expert builder of replica early aeroplanes, indicated that a reproduction biplane could provide much of the excitement of operating a classic aircraft at much lower cost and with greater practicality. Naturally, the Flycatcher was an obvious choice for a scion of the Fairey family.

At this point, in 1976, Fairey became aware of the beginnings of a Flycatcher replica project that had stalled when the original owner died. At that time, no more than a basic rear fuselage structure and some machined parts had been completed.

With the project acquired and John Hall engaged to complete the construction, work began in early 1977. Only around a quarter of the original drawings could be located, although the original 'Technical Publication'

1. This section is chiefly based on three articles written by John Fairey and published in The Aeroplane in March 1982, April 1982 and September 1991.
2. Fairey, J.S., Flying the Flycatcher, Aeroplane Monthly September 1991 p.547.

John Fairey's replica Flycatcher G-BEYB wearing the colours of 405 Flight, HMS Glorious *air group, in the air over Calshot on 26 June 1982. (Adrian Balch, Photair Press)*

The replica Flycatcher during its first public display at Middle Wallop, where the large grass airfield proved an ideal testing ground, on 28 July 1979. (Adrian Balch, Photair Press)

and rigging notes were available (see Chapters 4 and 7), and ex-Fairey employee and historian Ian D. Huntley provided photographs of Flycatchers under construction.[3]

Unfortunately, no authentic Armstrong-Siddeley Jaguar engine was available as very few of these engines survive. Fairey chose in its place a Pratt & Whitney R-985 Wasp Junior 14B model offering 400 hp in flight and 450 hp for takeoff, giving slightly more power than the original engine as well as being lighter and more reliable.

As a result of this necessary compromise, Fairey elected to complete the build without sacrificing its practicality for modern use, rather than slavishly following 1920s practices. The reproduction Flycatcher was therefore built as closely as reasonably possible to the original Flycatcher, but using alternative materials and systems where appropriate. This included installing DH Rapide undercarriage legs in place of the Fairey patent oleo-pneumatic units, which would have been difficult if not impossible to manufacture. The wheels were sourced closer to home than Fairey was expecting – two Lagonda V12 wire-spoked wheels he found in his garage happened to fit well, needing only some modifications to the hubs. Fairey decided to fit brakes to the wheels, unlike the original aircraft, but these proved so ineffectual they were later removed.

Particular care was taken to reproduce the flying surfaces and controls, including the all-important 'camber changing gear', to ensure that the replica flew in an identical fashion to the original. The differential elevator was also reproduced faithfully, though Fairey felt that its effect on the aircraft's longitudinal control was not particularly noticeable.

3. Fairey, J.S., Flycatcher Facsimile (part 1), Aeroplane Monthly March 1982 p.131.

The Flycatcher replica first flew in July 1979, wearing the colours of S1287 of 405 Flight, part of HMS *Glorious*' air group. Fairey reported that the replica was "docile but very powerful," controls were "powerful and effective", and "take-off and initial climb are spectacular".[4]

Interestingly, Fairey felt that the ailerons were very heavy to operate, which seemed to match the opinions of those who flew the aircraft later in its career,[5] if not those of the pilots originally testing it. This is unsurprising, considering the fact that the ailerons are full-span and unbalanced, so it is possible that the pilots conducting the initial testing were used to heavier aileron control. According to John Fairey, the heaviness of the ailerons prevented tidy slow rolls and barrel rolls. However, he reported that "loops and stall-turns are straightforward", as were half-rolls off the top. The differential operation of the ailerons also meant that there was no adverse yaw to contend with.

The 'camber changing gear' was found to be most effective at reducing the stalling speed when set at +10°, allowing the aircraft to land at the remarkably low speed of 36 kt, not a great deal faster than the top speed of the Furious-class carriers. Fairey remarked that "into-wind landings are straightforward and the aircraft has little tendency to bounce whatever its attitude on touch-down, provided that some effort is made to arrest the descent before impact".

The replica also exhibited excellent spinning characteristics. Although spin rate was rapid, it stopped spinning instantaneously when standard recovery action was applied.[6]

The Flycatcher delighted airshow crowds for 16 years until it was retired to the Fleet Air Arm Museum, Yeovilton in 1996. The last flight of the last flying Flycatcher was on 5 June 1996.

---

4. Fairey, J.S., Flycatcher Facsimile (part 2), Aeroplane Monthly March 1982 p.213.
5. See Nesbitt-Dufort, J., Open Cockpit: Flying Pre-War Fighting and Training Aircraft, p.32.
6. Fairey, J.S., Flycatcher Facsimile (part 2), Aeroplane Monthly March 1982 p.215.

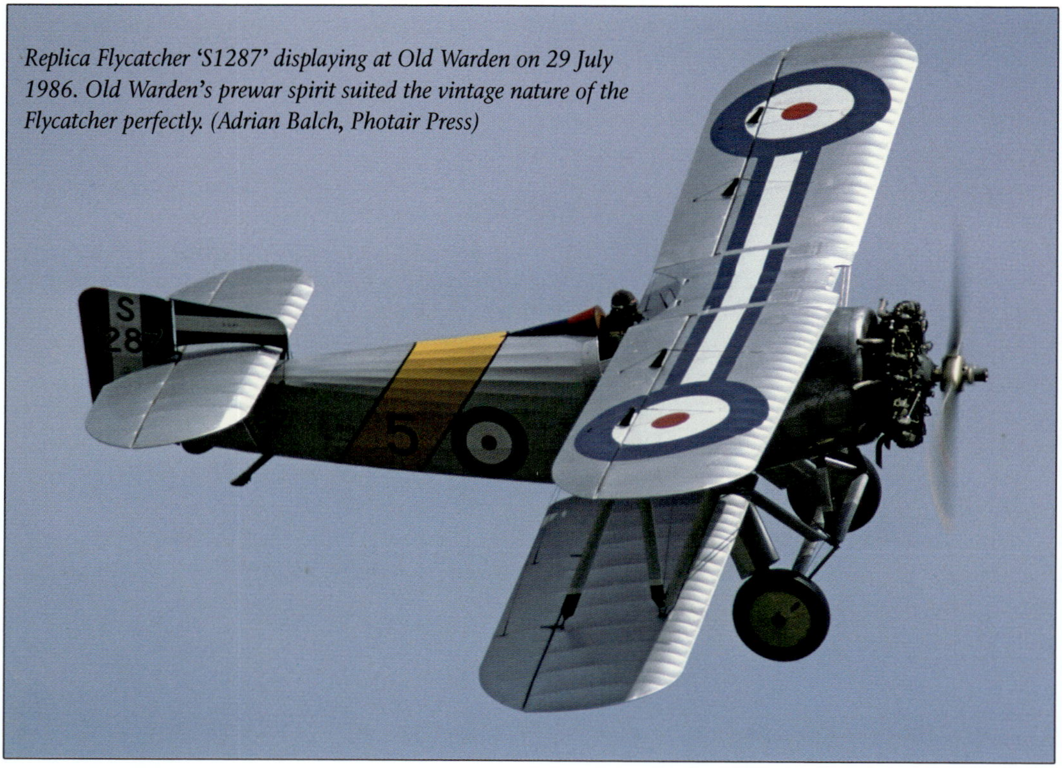

Replica Flycatcher 'S1287' displaying at Old Warden on 29 July 1986. Old Warden's prewar spirit suited the vintage nature of the Flycatcher perfectly. (Adrian Balch, Photair Press)

Flycatcher description

Data drawn from *Flycatcher Rigging and Maintenance Notes*[1] and *Flycatcher, Jaguar IV engine, Air Publication*

Fuselage

Consisted of a front portion built up of steel tubes with flexible cross-bracing in the transverse panels only, and a rear wooden portion comprising four longerons and four transverse panels, each transverse panel being built rigidly without bracing. Besides this there were frames of a more usual type at the front and immediately before the stern post, giving six bays altogether. For all practical purposes, the upper centre section was integral with the fuselage front portion.

The front transverse panel comprised a riveted steel engine bearing plate.

All four longerons were untapered, i.e. the cross section was square and constant throughout. The upper and lower longerons on each side were parallel to each other, and the side struts were at right angles to top and bottom longerons. This construction simplified the rigging.

The tubes comprising the upper centre section were permanently bolted to the top longeron in four places, both side panels being diagonally braced.

Floatation gear, comprising six rubberised fabric bags, were installed in the rear fuselage and upper decking.

Landing gear

For land work and for alighting on a ship's deck an oleo type undercarriage was fitted, this landing gear being interchangeable with an amphibian gear comprising a pair of floats, each one being fitted permanently with a landing wheel. [NB the duralumin V-bottom floats used towards the end of the Flycatcher's career were not fitted with wheels].

The wooden floats were 'boat-built' with a double skin of mahogany planking, with fabric between, laid over laminated rock elm frames and attached with brass pins. The wheels fitted to amphibian undercarriage were 650mm x 125mm.

In the land undercarriage almost the whole of the initial shock of landing was absorbed by the oil in the oleo leg, the compression rubber serving only to limit gradually the travel of the oleo leg, and to take the weight of the standing aircraft. In order to ensure that on rebound the oil would follow the rapid movement of the piston, an air bottle was provided. In action, the air in the upper portion of the air bottle was compressed while landing shocks were absorbed and on rebound the oil was forced by the compressed air to follow the movement of the piston.

The 'hardness' of the oleo leg could be adjusted to accommodate variations of temperature and load by moving a lever. This lever controls a valve in the piston which slid in the oil cylinder of the oleo leg.

The land undercarriage could be easily detached.

Tail plane

The tail plane was hinged about its front spar, the bolts attaching the spar to the fuselage and to the bracing tube on either side forming the hinges.

Main planes

The main planes for each side comprised one upper and one lower plane, held together by bracing wires arranged 'in a rather unusual manner', and one group of struts permanently assembled in the form of the letter 'N'.

For shipboard use the planes could be rapidly detached and again assembled in position.

The dihedral was 4° for the upper plane, while the lower plane possessed no dihedral angle.

The angle of incidence was 3° throughout both upper and lower planes. Slight adjustment was possible by means of the landing wires, but adjustment was barely necessary. The stagger was 2ft 8in at the centre section.

1. AIR 10/1233, National Archives.

Tail plane incidence gear

This was controlled by the hand wheel on the right hand side of the pilot's cockpit *[pulling on a wire running to a bobbin on a vertical actuating tube in the sternpost]*. The limiting positions of the tail plane were +4° and -2°. The handwheel required approximately 5 ¼ clockwise turns to move the tail plane from maximum to minimum incidence. A dial on the dashboard worked automatically informed the pilot of the position of the tail plane at any given moment.

Camber gear and ailerons

Both upper and lower main planes were hinged at the rear spar, thus forming four one-piece wing flaps which acted in the dual capacity of camber flaps and ailerons. They can be raised or lowered at the trailing edge by turning a crank in the cockpit, mounted below the instrument panel, which actuated the flaps through worm and nut. The handle required six turns in an anti-clockwise direction to raise from normal to position of minimum camber, and eighteen turns clockwise to lower the trailing edge to position of maximum camber. The position of the flaps at any moment was shown on a dial on the instrument panel in the same manner as the dial for the tail plane incidence.

[The handle turned a worm screw that raised or lowered a longitudinal tube hinged at the rear on which the control column is mounted. The aileron/camber wires were in a continuous loop so that raising the lever had the effect of feeding through the wires that elevate the ailerons while pulling on the wires that lower them. The ailerons operated in the normal way, but with all four in a lower position. In addition to lowering the ailerons to increase lift, they could also be raised slightly to reduce drag].

The principle of differential ailerons was incorporated in a small degree into this design.

Rudder

The rudder was controlled by separate pedals in place of the more normal rudder bar. The pedals were adjustable to the height of the pilot and were interconnected by a balancing cable passed over pulleys. An adjustable control lever was fitted to the port rudder pedal bearer, which cancelled out the pilot's need to maintain constant pressure on the rudder to counteract airscrew torque.

The elevators were rigged with 'cam-operated proportional elevator movement'. When the control column was close to the central fore-and-aft position, small movements produced small movements of the elevators but as the column moved further from central, small movements of the control column produce correspondingly larger movements of the elevators.

A larger fin and rudder were provided for when the aircraft was rigged as an amphibian/floatplane.

Tail skid

Rubbers in compression were used for absorbing shock. The skid was non-steerable but was free to swivel when the aircraft was being taxied.

Petrol system

Fuel was fed to the carburettor by gravity. The main feed pipe, fitted with a cock controlled by a rod and wheel in the pilot's cockpit, was in communication with a filter, the petrol flowing then direct to the carburettor. The whole petrol supply could be rapidly jettisoned in an emergency.

Trim

Some Flycatchers had a tendency to fly port-wing down. This could be corrected by introducing wash-in (3°20) to the port and wash-out (2°40) to the starboard planes.

Armament

The Flycatcher was armed with two .303in Vickers machine guns mounted on brackets on the fuselage sides, firing through the airscrew disc with the aid of Constantinesco-Colley (CC) synchronisation gear.

The gun brackets were adjustable in elevation, via a handle on the rear of the bracket, and azimuth, by adjustable bolts.

A camera-gun could be fitted on the Port-lower mainplane or in place of one of the Vickers guns.

Bomb racks carrying 25lb bombs could be fitted beneath each lower mainplane.

Flycatcher colours

All Flycatchers left the Fairey factory in all-over silver dope on the fabric-covered surfaces and bare metal cowling panels. Serial numbers were generally stencilled on the rear fuselage and repeated on the rudder, or occasionally the tail fin. Red-white-blue roundels were applied in six positions, and the rudder was generally marked in vertical blue-white-red bands.

Factory-finish included stencils showing lifting and trestle points, but photographs indicate that these were mostly removed in service use.

The Fleet Fighter Flights adopted identifying markings with the basic colours indicating which carrier's air group the aircraft belonged to, but displaying considerable variation and creativity across the Flights. The colours associated with each air group were as follows:

- HMS *Argus* – Green
- HMS *Courageous* – Light Blue
- HMS *Eagle* – Black
- HMS *Furious* – Red
- HMS *Glorious* – Yellow
- HMS *Hermes* – White

The colours could be represented by fuselage bands, vertical or sloping in either direction, coloured upper decking, chevrons or coloured numbers. The variety of markings carried by Flycatchers, considering the small numbers of aircraft built, and units they served with, is astonishing, and too broad to be listed here. To find the most comprehensive list of colour schemes during this period, the reader is recommended to study *Fleet Air Arm Aircraft, Units and Ships 1920 to 1939* by Ray Sturtivant and Dick Cronin, published by Air Britain. A selection of Flycatcher colour schemes is presented in the colour section of this book, see page 84.

Flycatcher data

First flight: 28 November 1922
Declared obsolete for all purposes: 1934
Length: 22 ft 10 in
Span: 29 ft
Height: 10 ft
Weights: Empty - 2,136 lb, Tare - 2,193 lb, Loaded - 3,030 lb (Jaguar IV)
Max speed: 133 mph at 5,000 ft (Jaguar IV)
Max altitude: 21,000 ft (Jaguar IV)
Climb rate: 5,000 ft - 3 mins, 10,000 ft - 8 mins (Jaguar IV)
Endurance: 1 hour 50 mins at 10,000 ft + 30 mins at ground level
Powerplant: 1 Armstrong Siddeley Jaguar III, 325 hp or Jaguar IV, 385 hp
(Prototypes only - Bristol Jupiter IV 400 hp)

Flycatcher in detail

The replica Flycatcher at the Fleet Air Arm Museum, displaying the type's characteristic posture, and showing the unusual dihedral on the upper wing and flat lower wing. (Author)

A starboard aspect of the replica Flycatcher at the Fleet Air Arm Museum. The nose is slightly longer than on the original aircraft, as the Pratt & Whitney Wasp engine fitted to the replica is somewhat lighter than the Armstrong Siddeley Jaguar that equipped the original. On production Flycatchers, the firewall was just ahead of the forward undercarriage strut mounting point. (Author)

The replica Flycatcher's undercarriage. A comparison with the image on page 5 representing prototype N163 indicates how closely the replica follows the original pattern. Note the easily-detachable linkages to enable the landplane undercarriage to be converted to floatplane configuation. (Author)

The replica Flycatcher's undercarriage from the other side. (Author)

Lower interplane strut and landing wire attachment on Flycatcher replica S1287. (Author)

Upper interplane strut and flying wire attachment on Flycatcher replica S1287. The rectangular 'hard point' at the forward strut attachment differs from the original Flycatcher arrangement which does not have a visible panel like this one. (Author)

The Flycatcher's tail assembly, seen from above the tailplane. The tailplane had a variable incidence, adjustable via a worm screw under the leading edge, hence the relatively large gap around the bottom of the fin. (Author)

The tail assembly from the underside of the tailplane, showing the hinge point of the variable-incidence mechanism. The push-pull rod for the elevator adjustment can also be seen, along with the control cables for the rudder. (Author)

An aft view of the replica Flycatcher at the Fleet Air Arm Museum, once again demonstrating the dihedral on the upper wing and the flat lower wing. (Author)

The starboard side of the cockpit opening. The sliding panel follows the original pattern, while the tall windscreen matches those of later aircraft. Earlier aircraft had a lower, curved, one-piece windscreen with a much shallower slope (Author)

The cockpit area seen from port, including the sliding side panel, windscreen and headrest. The instrument panel did not follow the arrangement of the original aircraft. (Author)

The starboard cowling panels removed to show the interior of the cockpit. The steel-tube construction of the forward fuselage, which formed a unit with the upper and lower wing centre sections, is apparent. Behind the pilot's seat, the wooden rear fuselage structure can be seen, including the diamond-braced frames which did away with the need for wire bracing in those components. (Author)

The port wings, seen from ahead. Note the twin control horns for the full-span, 'variable camber' ailerons. (Author)

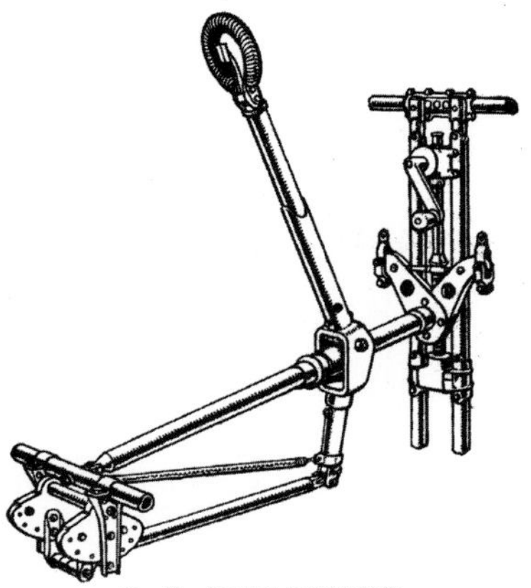

Fig. 38.—Control column unit.

An illustration of the control column from the Flycatcher Rigging Notes, showing how the shaft on which the column is mounted can be raised and lowered with the crank handle below the instrument panel, and which allowed the ailerons to droop, acting as flaps, while still functioning in the normal way. ('Flycatcher Rigging and Maintenance Notes', Air Publication 1078, Air Ministry, 1927)

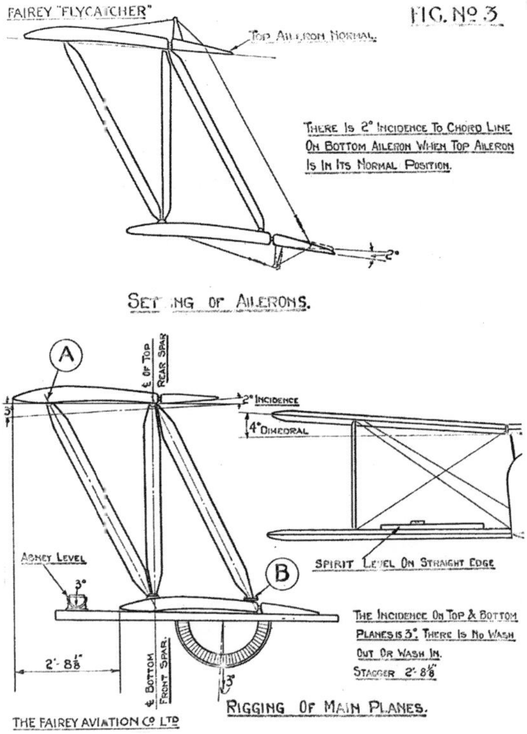

Dihedral, incidence and stagger of Flycatcher mainplanes. ('Flycatcher Rigging and Maintenance Notes', Air Publication 1078, Air Ministry, 1927)

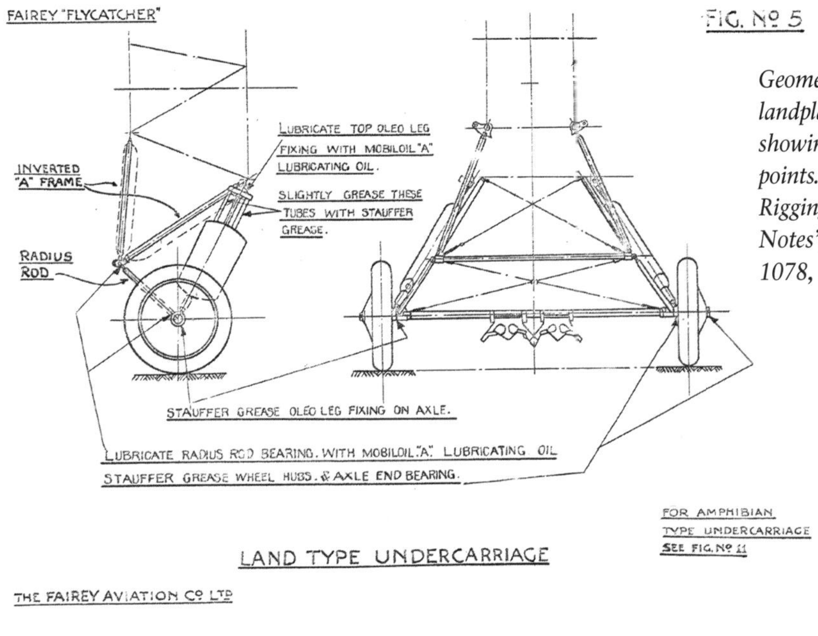

Geometry of Flycatcher landplane undercarriage, showing lubrication points. ('Flycatcher Rigging and Maintenance Notes', Air Publication 1078, Air Ministry, 1927)

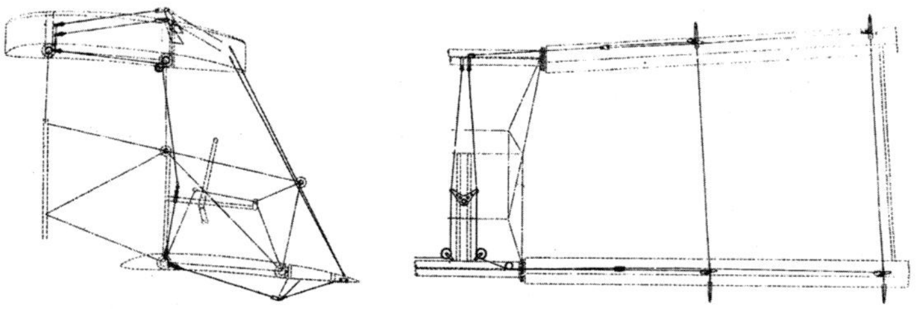

The cable runs for the ailerons and 'camber changing gear', showing the closed-loop circuit that allowed the ailerons to act as flaps. ('Flycatcher Rigging and Maintenance Notes', Air Publication 1078, Air Ministry, 1927)

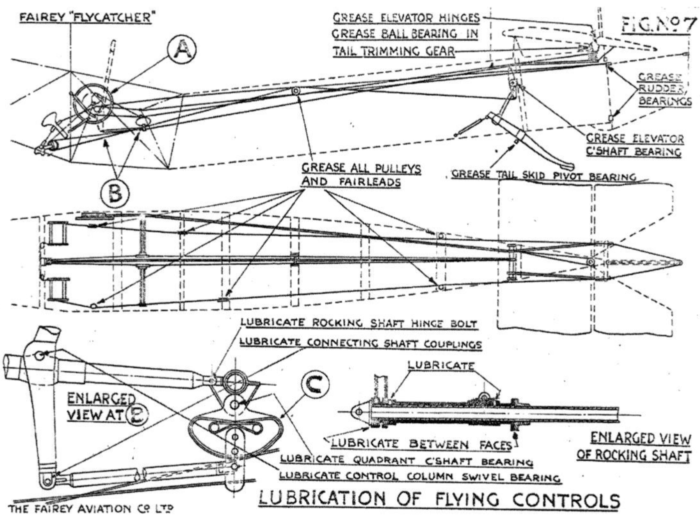

The Flycatcher's flying controls showing cable runs for rudder and elevator, and the control column bearings. ('Flycatcher Rigging and Maintenance Notes', Air Publication 1078, Air Ministry, 1927)

Controls of the Flycatcher's innovative aileron arrangement, showing the crank used to adjust camber. ('Flycatcher Rigging and Maintenance Notes', Air Publication 1078, Air Ministry, 1927)

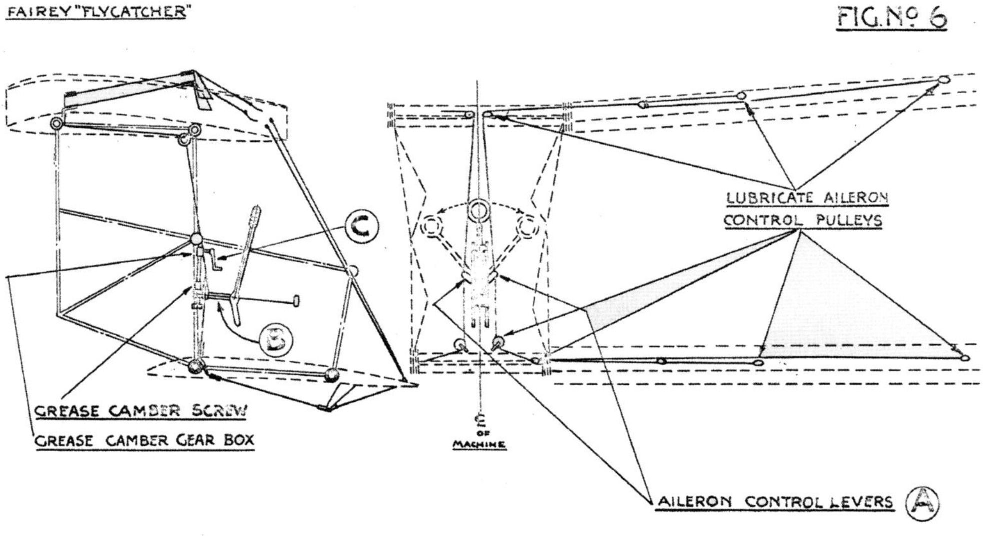

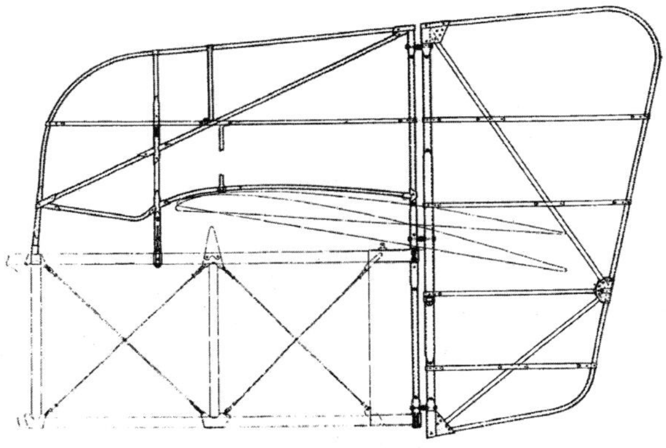

FIG. 22.—AMPHIBIAN FIN AND RUDDER.

The structure of the larger amphibian/floatplane fin and rudder, which could be fitted in place of the usual landplane tail assembly. The full upper and lower limits of the variable-incidence tailplane are marked. ('Flycatcher Rigging and Maintenance Notes', Air Publication 1078, Air Ministry, 1927)

FIG. 26.—CENTRE PLANE END RIB

FIG. 27.—CENTRE PLANE CENTRAL RIB

One of the Flycatcher's innovative aspects was the amount of metal in its structure. The wing centre-section ribs were formed from tubular upper and lower flanges with a sheet steel web, with holes cut for the spars to pass through, and for lightening. ('Flycatcher Rigging and Maintenance Notes', Air Publication 1078, Air Ministry, 1927)

The arrangement of the pilot's cockpit, showing the control column, throttle quadrant, pilot's seat and rudder pedals. The front view shows the layout of the instrument panel with the crank handle for adjusting wing camber. ('Flycatcher Rigging and Maintenance Notes', Air Publication 1078, Air Ministry, 1927)

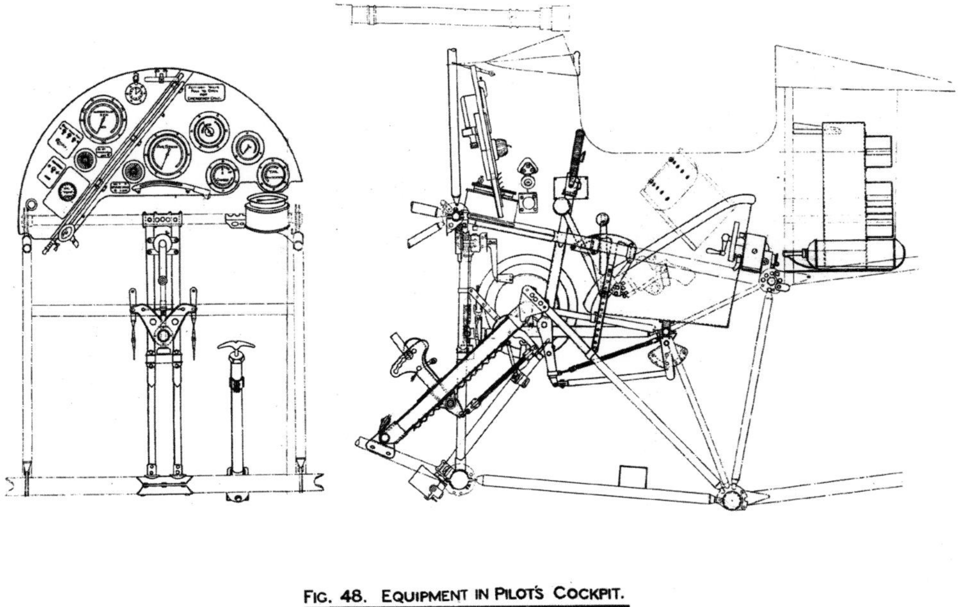

FIG. 48. EQUIPMENT IN PILOT'S COCKPIT.

Aircraft in factory finish, (see also page 76).
N9928 was part of the Miscellaneous Flight at RAF Hal Far, Malta until June 1930 before transferring to 401 Flight, HMS Courageous. *It was photographed flying over HMS* Eagle *in the Mediterranean sporting these unusual markings on the rear fuselage decking, thought to be in the green Air Group colour usually associated with HMS* Argus.

Aircraft in factory finish.
N9908/ '2' operated as a floatplane from HMS Hermes *when on the China Station with 403 Flight in 1926-7. The white fuselage band and tilted square containing the side number indicate an aircraft belonging to* Hermes' *air group.*

Aircraft in factory finish.
An early Flycatcher, N9680/ '1' first flew in December 1923 and went to its first front-line fighter Flight, 401 Flight, HMS Argus with the Atlantic Fleet, by February 1924. It is in this guise that N9680 is seen here, with green fuselage band and code number 1.

Aircraft in factory finish.
A Flycatcher of 403 Flight during its spell attached to the 5th Cruiser Squadron, made up of HMS Berwick, HMS Cornwall, HMS Cumberland, HMS Kent *and* HMS Suffolk, *from 1930. The identity of the aircraft is unknown, as it wore no serial on its fuselage or fin. It did, however, carry the Tudor Rose emblem of* HMS Cumberland *and a red and white chequered upper centre-section.*

Upper view of S1274 showing the individual markings, and a view of the standard layout of Flycatcher lower wing undersides with roundels as applied at the factory.

Left and opposite page:
Aircraft in factory finish.
401 Flight joined the air group of HMS Furious *in 1932, where S1274/ '527' gained its individual markings as seen here. The Flight's aircraft all wore the black fin with red diagonal stripe edged with white, and red fuselage band incorporating the side number, but S1274 also had red wing tips to denote a Flight-leader's aircraft.*

Aircraft in factory finish.
A relatively well-photographed but plainly marked Flycatcher from the first full production batch. The aircraft served as an uncoded floatplane, as seen here, at Kalafrana, Malta. The only concession to individuality in the markings is the black band around the rear half of the spinner.

Aircraft in factory finish.
S1273/ '2' was the first of the penultimate batch of Flycatchers to be ordered, and was delivered in January 1929. It is seen here wearing the blue fuselage band of HMS Courageous *during its second spell with 401 Flight, in 1931. The following year it collided with N9697 and was lost.*

Aircraft in factory finish.
N9889/ '8', another aircraft of 403 Flight, HMS Hermes *while on the China Station in 1926-7. Note the variation on the white Air Group band and titled side number square compared with N9908. The aircraft was later to serve with 402 Flight,* HMS Eagle, *until at least 1930.*

Aircraft in factory finish. 402 Flight's black side-number squares gave way to a black chevron by 1926-7, as seen on N9954/ '7'. Unlike most Flights where the side numbers were painted on top of the air group colour, this aircraft appears to have had the code masked so it appears as the same silver dope as the fuselage. The signal flag numeral 7 is painted on the fin. This aircraft only served with one front line Fighter Flight, No. 402, but went on to a number of shore stations.

Aircraft in factory finish. An extravagantly coloured Flycatcher of 404 Flight, HMS Courageous, N9679/ '13', while with the Mediterranean Fleet in 1929. The entire upper deck is painted in the air group colour of blue, outlined in white, while the forward-raking fuselage band is also outlined in white. The fuselage serial is somewhat non-standard being smaller and squarer than the factory-applied serial. This aircraft was lost in a collision with S1272 in February 1932.

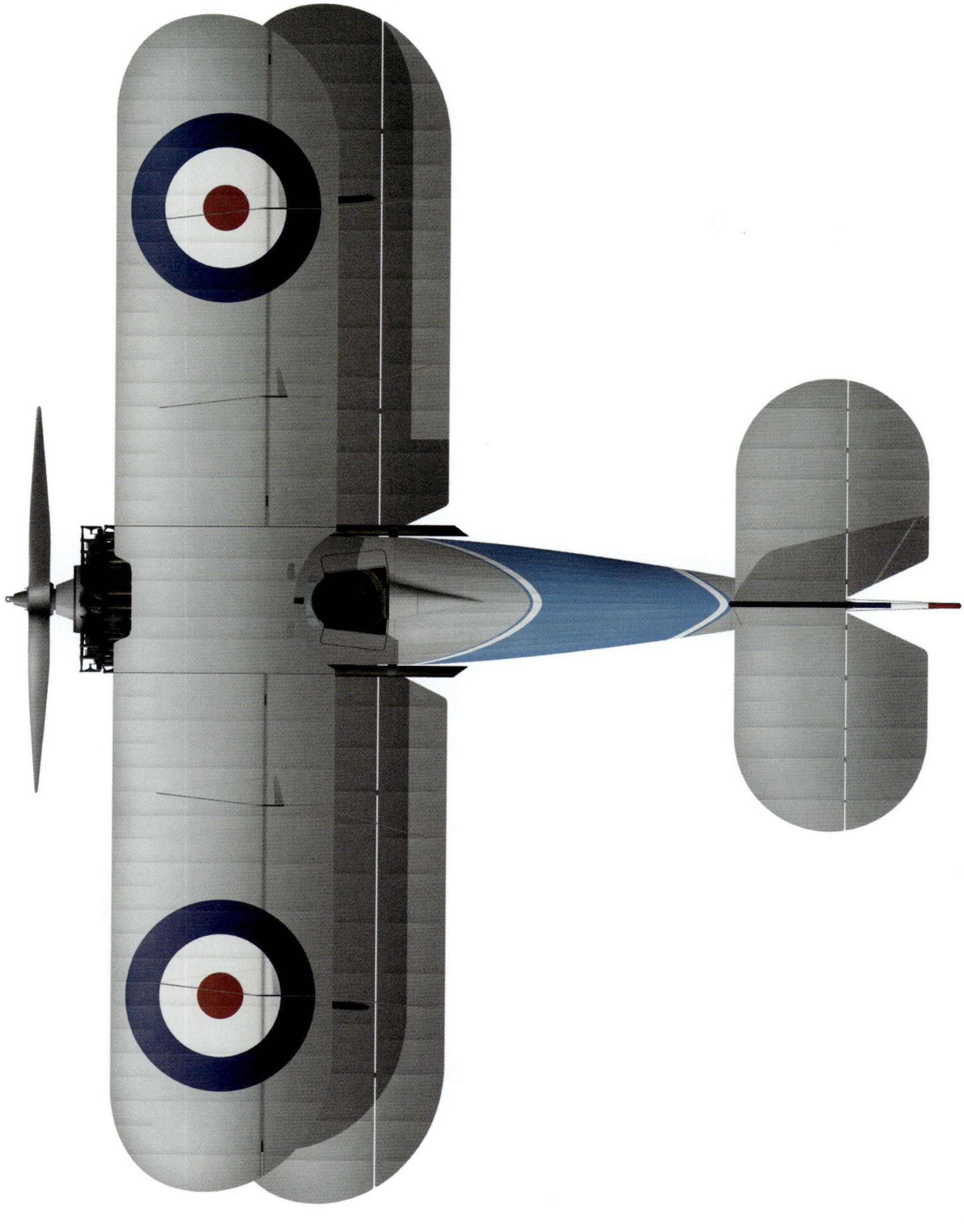

Left and opposite page: *Aircraft in factory finish.*
A long-lived Flycatcher late in its career, N9662/ '507' wears the highly raked blue fuselage band associated with HMS Courageous' *air group circa 1932. As the Flycatcher's career continued, the markings often became more elaborate. N9662's fuselage band is edged in white with a blue 'pinstripe', and the aircraft also has a black fin with the Flight's crest (which later became that of 800 Squadron).*

Flycatcher N9673 first flew in 1923, and spent several years of its life in trials and evaluation. It is seen here in 1932 as it appeared at the Marine Aeroplane Experimental Establishment, Felixstowe, for tests of duralumin floats with water rudders and an aluminium airscrew. It was plainly marked with no unit or air group insignia.

Aircraft in factory finish.
Flycatcher N9933/ '10' with 405 Flight, ashore, in July 1929 (probably at Hendon). The Flight was then part of HMS Furious' air group, hence the red fuselage band and fin. The Flight and its carrier were then part of the Home Fleet.

Aircraft in factory finish.
In 1930, 405 Flight transferred to the Mediterranean Fleet with HMS Glorious, and consequently changed its red fuselage bands for the yellow of Glorious' air group. S1293/ '19' is seen here during this phase. Note the unusually small characters of the serial on the rudder, which seemed to be a feature of aircraft from this carrier in the early 1930s.

Aircraft in factory finish.
This aircraft, N9669, flew with 405 Flight on HMS Furious *from September 1924. Intriguingly, though it does not wear any of the conventional Flight colours or markings, the naval signal flags on the tail read '4-0-5'. It retains all of the factory-applied stencils, which most service aircraft lost at some point during their lives*

S1277/ '1' while serving with 406 Flight aboard HMS Glorious *in 1931. The aircraft wears the yellow stripe of Glorious' air group, while the fin is black, bearing the winged trident emblem that would later be associated with 801 Squadron*

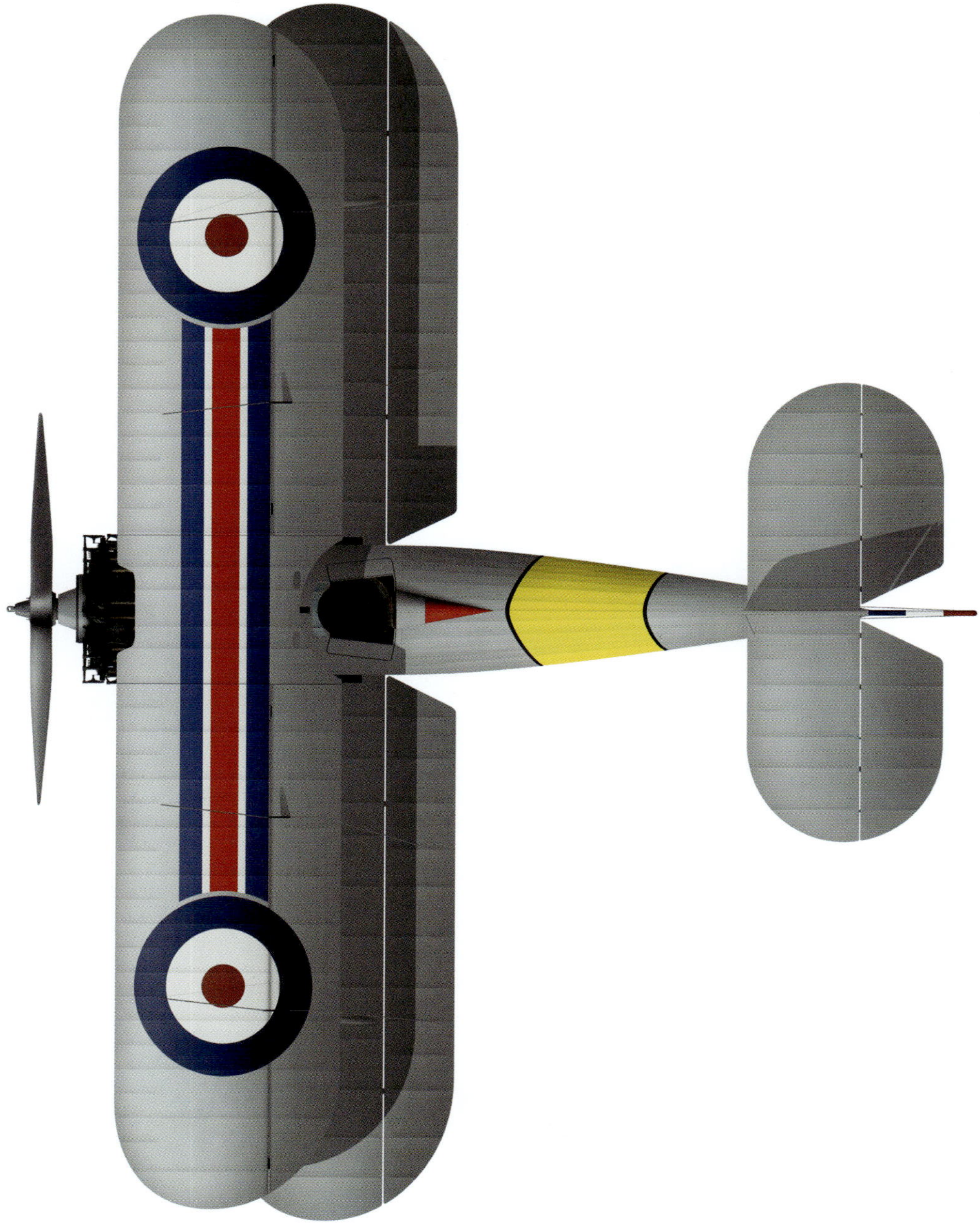

***Left and opposite page:** Aircraft in factory finish. Flycatcher S1280/ '3' operated from the B-turret platform of battleship* HMS Ramillies *of the 1*st *Battle Squadron in 1931. It continued to wear the yellow fuselage band of* HMS Glorious' *air group, as well as blue-red-blue stripes on the upper wing.*

Aircraft in factory finish. S1413 was from the last batch of Flycatchers to be ordered, specifically as catapult aircraft. For this reason, it has catapult spools fitted (see the inverted-v assembly beneath the rear fuselage). It also has the more modern duralumin floats that gradually supplanted the earlier wooden items. S1413 was delivered in 1930, and in 1932-3 served aboard the cruiser HMS Cumberland *with the 5*th *Cruiser Squadron*

Aircraft in factory finish. N9676 '10' *of 407 Flight,* HMS Courageous *air group, while based at Hal Far in Malta in 1928-29. As with N9679 of 404 Flight, the whole of the upper deck was blue, but in this case there was no 'pinstripe' to delineate the fuselage band from the upper deck, resulting in a 'half band' on the lower half of the fuselage. The aircraft had Flight-leader's streamers flying from the interplane struts.*

Aircraft in factory finish. N9950/'561' *was allocated to 405 Flight,* HMS Glorious, *in 1931, and the unit switched to three-digit codes the following year.* N9950 *remained with the Flight, mainly in the Mediterranean, until the Flight was combined with others to form 803 Squadron. As with* S1293, *the rudder serial is in unusually small characters.*